DESTINED TO MAKE AN IMPACT

Bishop Dr. Nicholas Duncan-Williams

DESTINED TO MAKE AN IMPACT
Bishop Dr. Nicholas Duncan-Williams

Unless otherwise note, all Scripture quotations are from the King James version of the Bible.

Originally published by Action Publications under the title, You Are Destined to Succeed (1990), Accra, Ghana.

ISBN – 1-56229-197-1

Pneuma Life Publishing, Inc.
4451 Parliament Place
Lanham, Maryland 20706
301-577-4052
http://www.pneumalife.com

Printed in the United States of America
1   3   5   7   9   10   8   6   4   2

Table of Contents

A PERSONAL WORD

There are numerous handicaps and weaknesses that life throws our way. For some, failure is due to natural circumstances. For others, a lost opportunity to succeed or prevail. This book comes to you with a very clear message of inspiration – YOU CAN SUCCEED IN THE NAME OF JESUS!

Time (and life) is no respecter of persons or position. Yet, what explains how and why some people are able to make adequate use of time to achieve laudable goals in life, even in the face of setbacks, handicaps, disabilities and weaknesses? The answer is in this book.

I, like King David. found out that, "For by thee I have run through a troop; and by my God have leaped over a wall," (Psalm 18:29). Succeeding in life starts with Christ. By the finger of God I rose above what was a hopeless situation.

Do not let your circumstances, where you come from and what people say about you, stop you from becoming what God has purposed for you. You too can have a story to tell if you believe God's words in this book.

Have there been times when you wondered what Christianity is all about? Probably you have asked a few questions that others ask: Is there such a thing as true Christianity? Can one succeed in life as a faithful Christian? Does faith in Christ really overcome the world? What is all this talk about prosperity? Does God really make his children prosperous? Is divine healing a reality today? Should you really aspire to succeed in life? If so, does God provide the resources through His word to enable you to achieve your goals?

Christianity is a mystery, and beyond all doubts, it is more than a religion. As a way of life it has attracted critics and detractors for nearly two thousand years. Yet, throughout history all the destructive devices wicked men have set up to wipe out Christianity have only served to accelerate its growth.

Still some ask, "Can it be that Christianity is something more than going to church? Is it God's purpose that you affect the world with your testimony of salvation in Christ? What is faith? Does it work?" Someone once told me, "I tried this faith stuff once and it did not work, so I stopped." Is this your stance on the subject? Are some of these questions on your mind?

Beloved, we can go on ad infinitum posing similar questions, which cry out for answers. Thank God, this book can provides answers to an infinite number of questions. It will present to you with tested keys to successful Christian living that are applicable anywhere on the surface of the earth. It is important that you begin to read with an open heart. Only in so doing may the Spirit of God impress upon you the precious truths that are written here. Do not be anxious, dear friend, for it is the Father's will that you succeed in life. I found out how; it is by God's grace.

May this book bring you a release and open new vistas of power for victory and success!

Chapter One

The Story of Salvation

Full-Gospel Christianity is more than a sophisticated biblical gimmick for fooling naïve country folks. It goes far beyond ritualistic dogmas. It is a way of life. Living in Christ is not a part-time occupation; in truth, it ought to be a lifetime experience. Salvation in Christ is not merely a mental assent to a sinner's prayer. There is more to it!

First of all, we must appreciate the fact that Christianity is not something to be used just in times of trouble, like a fire extinguisher. Rather, it is a lifetime commitment to God that gives one meaning and purpose for all of life, both physical and spiritual.

Let us go to the roots of the salvation story. Jesus was the first person to use the term born again. He was speaking to a top-flight religious official named Nicodemus when He said, "Except a man be born again he cannot see the kingdom of God"– (John 3:3). Nicodemus thought Jesus was talking about a second physical birth. Nicodemus' confusion is understandable, though, for as the Bible tells us, "... the natural man receiveth not the things of the Spirit of GOD" (1 Cor. 2:14). In a similar vein, the Bible says, "That which is born of the flesh is flesh; and that which is born of the Spirit is spirit," (John 3:6).

This last passage speaks of two realms, the physical and the spiritual. The physical realm deals with our senses – sight, smell, hearing, taste and touch. The spiritual realm is not detectable by any of our physical senses. It is achieved purely by faith.

Man is a spirit. He has a soul and lives inside a body. It is important to note that man without the new birth (in his present stage) is not what God created him to be. Man is in a fallen state, regardless of his education, status or influence (cf. Rom. 3:23).

IN THE BEGINNING

The story of salvation reaches back into the Garden of Eden in the Book of Genesis. God Himself created man in His own likeness. The Bible says emphatically, "And God created man in His own image, in the image of God created He him; male and female created He them" (Gen. 1:26-27). God called the first man Adam, and he, in turn, called his wife Eve. The Bible says God placed them in a beautiful garden, and charged them with the responsibility of cultivating and caring for it, while enjoying the fruits thereof: "And the LORD God took the man and put him into the garden of Eden to dress and keep it" (Gen. 2:15).

We have already established that God created man in His own image and after His likeness. In every sense of the word, man, at creation, was a direct replica of the Creator. Bear that in mind, because it is an extremely important fact and much depends on it.

The word likeness expresses the idea of "an exact replica or a duplication in kind". In other words, God duplicated

10

Himself in mankind. I believe that sounds a death knell for the doctrine of evolution and all the "monkey business" about man crawling around on all fours, balancing among the trees and suddenly walking upright. Man did not evolve from a monkey, but was originally made in the image of God, with all the full intellectual and spiritual capabilities.

God gave man supreme authority and dominion over the work of His hands, and this position was firmly enshrined in the following proclamations:

And let them have dominion over the fish of the sea, and the fowl of the air and over the cattle and over all the earth. (Genesis 1:26)

And God blessed them, and God said unto them, "Be fruitful, and multiply and replenish the earth and subdue it; and have dominion over ... every living thing that moveth on the earth." (Genesis 1:28)

Let us share a few insights about Adam's position in the whole framework of creation. It is evident from the scriptures above that God made him superior to the rest of creation. As both a physical and a spiritual being, God placed man directly under His under authority, and further placed all other creation under man's. Adam was god over the earth (see Hebrews 2:6-7). He was subordinate only to God.

Theologians suggest that the key to a total understanding of the Bible lies within its first chapters, which I believe without reservation. Let us examine a few more incidents in the Garden of Eden. Along with the glory, splendor and majesty of Adam's position, God laid down a few clearly irrevocable do's and don'ts concerning their relationship and fellowship, and Adam's modus operandi.

11

THE FALL

We read in Genesis 2:16-17 that:

> *And the LORD God commanded the man, saying, Of every tree of the garden thou mayest freely eat: but of the tree of the knowledge of good and evil, thou shalt not eat of it: for in the day that thou eatest thereof thou shalt surely die.*

I want you to observe and note the word commanded. Sure enough, what God has commanded must be obeyed. That, uncompromisingly, is His immutable word and it remains so today. God has commanded all men to repent and be born again,

> *And the times of this ignorance God winked at; but now commandeth all men every where to repent.* (Acts 17:30)

> *Verily, verily, I say unto thee, Except a man be born again, he cannot see the kingdom of God... Marvel not that I said unto thee, Ye must be born again.* (John 3:3, 7)

The Bible makes no secret of the fact that Adam missed the mark. In fact, it was something much more than that. Adam and his wife, Eve, ate of the forbidden fruit from the tree of the knowledge of good and evil –(Gen. 2:17; 3:16). In so doing, Adam disobeyed God. What he did was tantamount to high treason; he sold his birthright to Satan (1 Tim. 2:14). A sad commentary indeed!

Friend, what Adam and Eve did was more significant than just eating a piece of fruit. The issue here was disobedience to God's word, which undermined Adam's superior position in the economy of God, and this had deep and far-reaching spiritual implications.

God commanded Adam to subdue the earth and have dominion over all things. Do you realize that the snake was also a living creature? Adam could have exercised authority over it! After all, according to the Bible, Adam had already given names to all the creatures, including the snake (Gen. 2:19-20).

Man was created with a will. He was made a free moral being, accountable for all actions that did not line up with God's word. This is a crucial truth.

Allow the Holy Spirit to enlighten you with understanding. As you will see, there were both physical and spiritual consequences to Adam's disobedience.

Just as God had decreed, Adam died (Gen. 5:5; Matt 24:5). In the Garden of Eden, Adam died spiritually the moment he sinned, passing from immortality to mortality. The penalty of death had been pronounced. As a result, about 930 years later, Adam died physically as well. Sin has a wage called "death," and Adam had to pay the price in full, no matter how long it took.

In his book, Newborn, Harold M. Freligh makes an interesting comment on the story of Adam. He says, "Spiritually man is dead. The spirit of man is like the top story with a skylight that opens to heaven. When Adam fell, this part of his being died at once, he had blackout. That is why when God came down to the garden, Adam ran to hide. There was no spiritual response to God's fellowship. There was fear instead. This dreadful tragedy was passed on to Adam's entire posterity." The Bible says "Wherefore, as by one man sin entered into the world, and death by sin; and so death passed upon all men for that all have sinned" (Rom. 5:12).

Adam died in spirit and later in body. In the spirit, he was alienated from God; he shifted from the realm of faith to the realm of sight. Adam could no longer understand spiritual things. His spiritual inclinations were lost. Whereas at creation Adam had been given dominion over this world, he had now lost his power, authority and dominion to Satan. Thus, Satan became the god of this world. In 2 Corinthians 4:4, the Bible says: "... the god of this world hath blinded the minds of them which believe not ..." Satan is shown here as god of this world.

This point is emphasized in Luke's account of the temptation of Jesus in Luke 4:6. "All this power will I give them and the glory of them: for that is delivered unto me: and to whomsoever I will I give it." There is no account that Jesus disputed the validity of this overwhelming statement. It was a direct consequence of Adam selling out to Satan.

Adam's fall affected man physically, too. Poverty, disease, aging and all other kinds of afflictions have since affected and disturbed the human race down through the ages.

The famous American Charismatic Bible teacher, Dr. Kenneth Hagin, elaborates on this point:

Spiritual death is that which lays hold of our spirits then or bodies. Physical death is a manifestation of spiritual death. The second death is the ultimate finality of death, or the home of the spiritual dead.

As Dr. Hagin stated, spiritual death came to earth first, then manifested itself in the physical body by destroying it.

Just as Satan became Adam's new master and lord, we, too, are born in submission to the devil and his evil manipulations. In Romans 6:16, the Bible explicitly states,

Know ye not, that to whom ye yield yourselves servants to obey, his servants ye are to whom ye obey; whether of sin unto death, or of obedience unto righteousness?

Just like a small drop of poison can contaminate a person's system, so the deadly virus of sin entered mankind's spirit when man fell and every part of his being became contaminated. Thus, mankind has been spiritually enslaved to Satan.

How can man escape this bondage? The answer lies in an "Emancipation Proclamation" that God declared for us in heaven.

Chapter Two

Emancipation
Proclamation

Forced slavery is a detestable and an abominable act of mankind. It is a cruel system whereby one person becomes another's chattel. In a spiritual sense, that is what man became after the Fall; that is, a slave to Satan, sin and sickness.

The world undoubtedly knows more than one kind of slavery. Physical slavery in some form or another has also been practiced throughout the ages. Historically, this institution has proliferated in Africa, the Middle East, India, China, Rome and Greece, and most recently and notoriously, in the Americas. Yet today, physical slavery, for the most part, is no longer considered acceptable in the world.

An examination of how this development was achieved can offer us an insight into how to free ourselves from our own bondage to Satan.

In 1808, as a result of mounting international condemnation of human slavery, both the United States and Britain outlawed the African Slave Trade. By 1840, the practice was completely abolished in the British colonies. France as well later freed the slaves in its colonies in 1848.

Although other countries continued to rely on practice of slavery in the Central and South American colonies, the struggle between abolitionists and slave owners reached a climax in 1860 with the outbreak of the American Civil War. As slavery became the central issue in the conflict, which threatened to destroy the United States, President Abraham Lincoln was forced to take a stand. In 1863, in a single paragraph of a speech, the President announced what has become known as the "Emancipation Proclamation," freeing all American slaves from that day forward.

Soon, the tide began to turn in favor of Lincoln's forces. By 1865, the Union Army had prevailed and the adoption of the thirteenth amendment to the U.S. constitution officially completed the abolition of American slavery. The price of freedom had been paid with the blood of American soldiers.

When Adam and Eve disobeyed God and ate of the tree, they immediately became the slaves of disobedience and the devil. That single act of disobeying God meant that they had obeyed the devil. Thus, by choice, they became slaves to sin. This principle is shown in Romans 6:16:

> *Know ye not, that to whom ye yield yourselves servants to obey, his servants ye are to whom ye obey; whether of sin unto death, or of obedience unto righteousness?*

In essence, the spirits of Adam and Eve were transformed from the likeness or image of God to the likeness of their new master, the devil. All men born after Adam have had a sinful nature. Scripture corroborates this fact.

Mankind, the Bible says, is "... carnal, sold under sin" (Rom. 7:14). It says in Ephesians 2:1, "And you hath he quickened who were dead in trespasses and sin." In man, "dwelleth no good thing" (Rom. 7:18).

The willful disobedience of Adam and Eve was sin before God. Logically, before God could give back eternal life, someone had to pay the price to buy us back from the condition of slavery. The price of redemption required that it be a life for a life. Redemption was God's rescue operation.

REDEMPTION

In 1 Corinthians 6:20; 7:23, Paul defines redemption as being bought with a price. Just as the physical freedom of American slaves came by the blood of Union soldiers, our redemption came by the blood of Christ, who was sent on earth to achieve it for us. (Read also Isaiah 44:21; Matt 20:28; Heb 9:12; Gal 4:14.)

Christ did not die for His own sins, of course; He Himself was sinless. Second Corinthians 5:21 states that, "For he hath made him to be sin for us, who knew no sin; that we might be made the righteousness of God in Him." Jesus Christ willingly laid down His life at Calvary for the sins of mankind.

The apostle Paul wrote in 1 Corinthians 15:3, "...how that Christ died for our sins according to the scriptures". The crucifixion of Jesus Christ at Calvary was the supreme price of sin, paid to obtain eternal redemption for mankind (Heb 9:12).

From what is one redeemed? From the bondage of the Law and its curses; from the power of sin and the grave; and from all troubles, iniquity, evil, death, and destruction; from the shackles of satanic oppression, obsession, and possession. (Read Gal. 4:5; 3:13; Rom. 6:18; Psalm 49:15; Gen. 48:16.)

Through redemption, we have justification, forgiveness, adoption and purification; and Friend, believe that it is precious (Rom. 3:24; Eph. 1:17; Tit. 2:14). By redemption, God manifests His power, grace, love and compassion (Isa. 50:2; John 3:16).

When we are redeemed we become God's property, His first fruits, "a chosen generation, a royal priesthood, an holy nation, a precious people; that we should shew forth the praises of him who has called us out of darkness into His marvelous light" (1 Peter 2:9).

Almost two thousand year ago a solemn desolation resounded. Mankind was set free! Liberty had come! Freedom had been purchased! The debt was paid! Redemption was made complete! The curse was broken! Mankind's slavery to Satan was all over (Gal. 3:13-14)!

Oh, what good news! This is your emancipation proclamation. It is a valid declaration of freedom.

It is a "legal document" backed by all the authority and power of Heaven, condemning Satan's attempt to enslave you. Now it is up to you to believe it, confess it and act on it.

Rise up in the power of God's might and shout for joy, sin has no hold on you! Sickness has no power over you! The precious blood of His Son, Jesus Christ, bought your freedom. The curse is broken. Jesus Christ has saved you and lives in your heart. Jesus the Savior and Lord is your Emancipator and Liberator.

ARE ALL FREE?

In his book, Authority In Three Worlds, the American Bible teacher Charles Capps, made a captivating statement on salvation. He said, "There is only one way to Heaven. It is not through the church door. It is through Jesus the door! Jesus is the way!"

Jesus Christ the Son of God, gave His life for each of us: "For God so loved the world, that he gave His only begotten son that whosoever believeth in Him should not perish, but have eternal life" (John 3:16). Furthermore, Romans 5:6 tells us,

For when we were yet without strength, in due time Christ died for the ungodly.

Beloved friend, the Bible stands indisputably as the solid foundation for everything the Christian believes. What we feel or think is not always the truth, but the Word of God is TRUTH.

The divine arrangement for changing man's sinful nature back to the likeness of our Creator is being born again. As we saw in the case of Nicodemus (John 3:1-8), this concept cannot be understood in physical terms because it is a spiritual experience. Rather, the phenomenon occurs when you accept Jesus Christ as your Savior, asking Him to forgive you of your sins and to become Lord of your life.

Our generation has a misconception of what truth is. Truth has assumed many faces today. Humanism and intellectualism have imbedded themselves deep into the minds of many.

I do not dispute or ignore the scientific and technological breakthroughs of our day. But I stand firmly by the Word of God regardless of our degree of scientific advancement. No matter how high man progresses mentally, the Bible emphasizes that he is dead to the things of God. The Bible says in Rom 3:23, "For all have sinned, and come short of the glory of God."

Even the most educated men in the world, if they are not born again spiritually, still "... have their understanding darkened, being alienated from the life of God ..." (Eph. 4:18). Remember Nicodemus? Though he was an outstanding educational and legislative leader in his day, Jesus openly told him "Ye must be born again" (John 3:3). Secular education is necessary; academic excellence is indispensable; however, when it comes to the things of the spirit, they matter very little. A renowned Bible scholar once philosophized, "Education never takes a man higher than the top of his skull."

Today many have put their hope of salvation in church membership. What a fallacy! It is one thing to have one's name written on a church register, and another to have it in the Lamb's Book of Life. Millions cling to what they call "confirmation". If your faith is not based on your faith in Jesus Christ, even a church confirmation will be useless. You will be confirmed and, yet, condemned.

The whole doctrine of Confirmation seems to have been hijacked by the devil and he is using it to make people committed to church rather than to Christ. No confirmations will save your soul; only repentance and faith in the finished work of Jesus Christ will.

For others, baptism is the consolation. They would stretch out their unsaved necks and shout, "Bishop Nick, I am a Christian. I was baptized as a small baby."

That is another false ground upon which to stand. Renew your mind with the biblical truth that true baptism by water is a post-salvation and post-conversion experience. The fact is that, if you are not born again, no number, no formula, no mode of baptisms will save your soul. If anything, you will go into the water a dry sinner only to come out of the water a wet sinner.

At conversion, you die to sin (Rom 6:1-2), to self (Gal 2:20), and to the world (Gal 6:14). Thereafter you are baptized as commanded by Jesus in Matthew 28:19, to symbolize your identification with his death, burial and resurrection. So, then, baptism does not lead to salvation but is a visible sign of the change that has taken place inside.

Briefly, let me talk about religious ceremonies, such as ablutions, penance, prayer forms and the like. If these are not based on personal faith in the Lord Jesus, they become mere formalism. To substitute formalism for personal faith in Christ is to disapprove of His suffering on Calvary's cross (1 Cor. 1:18).

God is not willing that any of His creation should perish (2 Peter 3:9). The divine provision is that, "... whoever shall call on the name of the Lord shall be saved" (Acts 2:21). Salvation is for all (Mark 16:15). God requires that you believe His Word concerning the salvation of your soul when you hear or read it today (Heb 2:3).

This goes beyond any kind of mental assent to His Word or a memorization of scriptures. The Bible says that "... with the heart man believeth unto righteousness" (Rom 10:10). When you believe the word of God with your heart, it produces faith, a subject that I will deal with extensively later in this book.

Faith produces a corresponding action. Some Christians live under the erroneous belief that they will go to heaven no matter how they live. I personally disagree, because it does not stand to reason or logic. Your belief must correspond with your behavior. The infallible Word of God encourages born again Christians to walk in Christ (Phil. 2:5; 2 Cor 5:17).

Just imagine this. How can you as a born again believer saved, washed in the precious blood of Jesus and filled with

Holy Spirit of God and yet comfortably continue smoking, telling lies, fornicating, and engaging in all the things unbelievers indulge in? Where then is your witness? Where then is your light?

Unfortunately, many Christians know Jesus as Savior but not as Lord. "Is there a difference, Bishop Nick?" You may ask. Sure enough, there is a world of difference. If you accept Christ as Savior of your soul, then certainly you must live daily in total submission and obedience to His Word. His Word is His will for your life on earth in every situation. When you say, "Jesus is Lord," it is by implication a confession of submission. You are turning your life over to Him.

You must realize that when Jesus is Lord over your life, it means walking hand in hand with Him. There will be times when you get into difficult and thorny situations. The world and its divergent values may press in you. No matter what happens though, we cannot afford to compromise the Word of God.

Occasionally I have heard some Christians give flimsy excuses for their compromising stand. "Pastor, but you know the situation in which I find myself, I can't help it." "God understands me," they may add apologetically. Listen to me; God does not tolerate compromise. His Word says:

> *There hath no temptation taken you but such as is common to man: but God is faithful, who will not suffer you to tempted above that ye are able; but will with the temptation also make a way of escape, that ye may be able to bear it. (1 Corinthians10:13)*

Today, as always, God is calling for separation. Repent of your sins and accept the salvation of God through faith in Jesus Christ as his blood washes away your sins. Thus, you are saved by the grace of God (Eph.2: 8-9).

NEW POSITION

In the previous pages I gave you a personal word on salvation. We have in this chapter taken a look at God's "Emancipation Proclamation." That sounds big, doesn't it? Throughout this chapter, I have tried to show you how God has redeemed for us that which the devil stole. God has restored to His saints redeemed power, authority, glory, blessings, prosperity, health and peace in this life on earth.

Salvation in Christ is just the door through which one enters the mansion of goodness prepared by God. It is the first step on the way that leads one on a long journey by faith to the land of glory. Jesus, who is the DOOR, is also the WAY! You enter the DOOR to walk in the WAY.

The next chapter is a crucial one to your life. You are saved, but where do you go from here? There is such a thing as the faith LIFE (Rom.1: 17). God has a word for your new life. Colossians 1:13 affirm "He has delivered us from the power of darkness and translated us into the Kingdom of His dear Son." As a born-again Christian, you are a child of the Kingdom (Eph 2:19), and you must live in obedience to the divine law – God's Word.

Chapter Three

The Overcoming Faith

Faith is the master key into all God has for mankind. In the same way, unbelief is the bolt that forever shuts man out from God's presence and provision.

There is so much talk about faith among Christians today that sometimes its true significance is flawed. Today, Christian men and women, and even children, talk and preach about faith. Many claim to base their lives upon it. Yet, more often than not, there is a limited understanding of faith.

This chapter offers you some tremendous challenges vital to your solid understanding of the dynamics of faith.

The Bible makes no secret of the fact that, "the just shall live by faith" (Rom 1:17); and that without faith "it is impossible to please God" (Heb 11:6). Faith is what the born-again Christian lives by. Faith pleases God; and to please God, we must have faith.

Maybe you still have questions such as: What is faith? How does one acquire faith? Does faith increase and grow?

Are there different kinds of faith? Can I lose my faith? Do all men have faith? Your thorough comprehension of the answers to these questions will give you the overcoming faith that is so vital for life.

According to Harold Freligh, "Faith is that voluntary act and attitude of the individual whereby he places the weight of his need upon and governs his actions by a trusted object. In the scriptural realm the trusted "object" is God, and voluntary act induced by hearing and believing His word."

If any man has seen faith in action in this generation, surely it must be one of the "fathers" of the Charismatic movement, Dr. Oral Roberts. Let us see what he says about faith! What is there about faith that causes God's rewards to come to us? First of all, faith is the only thing that recognizes God for who He is.

We talk critically about faith without examining Hebrews 11. This chapter is sometimes called the "Hymn of Faith," just as 1 Corinthians 13 is known as the "Hymn of Love," and Genesis 1 as the "Hymn of Creation." Hebrews 11:1 states that:

> *Now faith is the substance of things hoped for, the evidence of thing not seen.*

The writer to the Hebrews helps us to understand that faith operates in a realm other than that of sight or outward tangible evidence. As we read in Mark 11:22, "Jesus answering saith unto them, Have faith in God!" Why? The reason is that the faith of God is eternal in essence, spiritual in substance, and unfathomable in scope. Glory to God! The faith of God sits high in the heavenlies. The faith of God is spiritual; everything about God is spiritual.

A new convert once stopped me in the church's corridor and asked. "Do you say God has given me faith?" There was a deep searching look in his eyes. I laid my hands on his shoulders and quickly assured him from Romans 12:3

"For I say, through the grace given unto me, to every man that is among, you, not to think of himself more highly than he ought to think; but to think soberly, according as God hath dealt to every man the measure of faith"

There is a natural faith just as there is supernatural faith. Natural faith is for natural things, but the God-kind of faith is a spiritual phenomenon. I explained to this young man, "The supernatural faith is God-ward and stands solely upon the Word of God regardless of any natural influences." He nodded his head and shouted with excitement, "Amen!"

THE CHARACTER OF FAITH

It will help you to read this chapter with spiritual understanding because timeless truths are involved. There are no obstacles between faith and God. Faith does not talk about or believe about Christ, but believes in and is centered solely on Him as God's eternal word. Remember, Jesus said that "the word that I speak unto you, they are spirit and they are life" (John 6:63).

Faith is not the same as hope. Faith gives substance to our hope (Heb 11:1). In other words, if you do not have hope, you have nothing for your faith to obtain. In the words of Dr. Fredrick K.C. Price, Senior Pastor of Crenshaw Christian Center, California, "If you have hope and do not have faith then you have nothing by which to obtain that which you hope for."

Faith is essentially related to every aspect of the Christian experience. It is related foremost:

29

To Repentance;

Testifying both to the Jews, and also to the Greeks, repentance toward God, and faith toward our Lord Jesus Christ. (Acts 20:21)

To Justification;

Therefore being justified by faith, we have peace with God through our Lord Jesus Christ; by whom also we have access by faith into this grace wherein we stand, and rejoice in the hope of the glory of God. (Rom 5:1)

To the preaching of the gospel,

For I am not ashamed of the gospel of Christ: for it is the power of God unto salvation to every one that believeth; to the Jews first, and also to the Greek. For therein is the righteousness of God reveal from faith to faith: as it is written, the just shall live by faith. (Rom 1:16-17)

To the written word,

But these are written, that ye might believe that Jesus is the Christ, the Son of God; and that believing ye might have life through His name. (John 20:31)

To obedience;

But now is made manifest, and by the scriptures of the prophets, according to the commandment of the everlasting God made known to all nations for the obedience of faith" (Rom 16:26).

To prayer

But without faith it is impossible to please him: for he that cometh to God must believe that He is, and that he is a rewarder of them that diligently seek him. (Heb 11:6)

Therefore I say unto you, what things soever ye desire, when ye pray, believe that ye receive them, and ye shall have them. (Mark 11:24)

Faith is not only a fact; faith is also an act. Your faith must be related to your works (James 2:14:26). By faith Christ indwells us "The Christ may dwell in your hearts by faith;

that ye being rooted and grounded in love ..." (Eph 3:17); it is by faith we receive the Holy Spirit "That the blessing of Abraham might come on the Gentiles through Jesus Christ through faith" (Gal 3:14). Faith clothes us in God's right-eousness after providing us the remission of sins:"And be found in him, not having my own righteousness, which is of the law, but that which is through the faith of Christ, the righteousness which is of God by faith,... To him give all the prophets witness, that through his name whosoever believeth in him shall receive remission of sins" (Phil 3:9; Acts 10:43).

Faith is the believer's blood lifeline. When faith stops flowing in the believer's life, be certain that spiritual death will follow. The fact that faith is the gift of God (Rom 12:3) does not preclude a need for willful determination on our part. The unwavering life of faith demands your daily watchfulness.

We can associate faith to a man riding a bicycle; he must not stop lest he falls down. Faith is not static; it is a virile, living principle. Commenting on the giant strides made in his ever-flourishing ministry, the late Archbishop Benson Idahosa of Nigeria said, "Faith is not timid, it has divine propelling force operating it."

FAITH IN ACTION

There are many spiritual lessons and messages on the successful operation of faith in the Bible. Recently God laid a deep impression on my heart that, "Faith will always find a way out." The spiritual lessons inherent in this message are many. Consider, for instance the narrative in Matthew 9:20-21;

> *And behold, a woman, which was diseased with an issue of blood twelve years, came behind, and touches the hem of his garment: for she said within herself, if I may but touch his garment, I shall be whole.*

31

Great lessons of faith lie beneath these precious scriptures. I have no doubt you have read or heard something about the woman with the issue of blood.

Faith always encounters hurdles and barriers, but it always manages to overcome them. In Mark's account of the same incident, he indicates that the woman with the issue of blood "had suffered many things of many physicians" (Mark 5:26). She might have sold all her possessions to obtain medical attention. Her life was ebbing away every day.

Then one day she heard about Jesus. There is one such day in every man's life, the day of divine visitation. Behold, today is the day God stills your tempest. The wretched woman heard that Jesus, the miracle worker was in town. She made up her mind firmly. With resolute confidence she said, "If I may but touch his garment, I shall be whole" (Matt 9:21).

This woman was despised, mocked and scorned. She was regarded as unwholesome and unclean. Undoubtedly, she was aware of people's negative attitude towards her. Prejudice, I believe, was her initial challenge to overcome.

The second obstacle that she had to overcome was the crowd. There will always be a greater number of people to foster discouragement than to cultivate encouragement and acceptance. Nevertheless, the woman's faith saw her through. If your faith is weak, then it is because your vision of Christ, the ultimate Source of your miracle, is blurred.

The woman set her eyes, mind and heart on Jesus. Everyone around Jesus had a need, but their doubt and unbelief stood in their way. Many were religious "window-shoppers". But, lo and behold, here came a woman with a resolute and overcoming faith.

As she stepped forward, the crowd predictably began to murmur, complain and cast contemptuous remarks. The Bible says she "...came from behind, and touched his garment" (Mark 5:27). The teeming, jostling crowd did not deter her from touching the hem of Jesus' garment. The faith that overcomes the world is the faith that does not respect hindrances. She kept moving toward Jesus Christ, and the crowds, seeing her determination, began to resist her. But her perseverance caused the crowd to draw back because she was not the kind that gave up. Faith keeps going. Halleluiah!

It is by keeping your eyes on Jesus that you will reach your goal. In a matter of time the afflicted woman stood behind Jesus, the Author of life. This was not the time for prayer and fasting, binding and loosing, my friend. After all, it was the prayer, fasting, binding and loosing which had brought her inches away from the HEALER. It was now time to act on the word she had heard and believed. It was time to put her faith into action.

Thanks to God, she knew better! She "...touched his garment" (Mark 5:7b). Jesus immediately felt virtue go out of Him, and demanded to know who had touched Him. Believe it, a single touch can make the difference. When He eventually saw the woman, He said to her in Matthew 9:22, "Daughter, be of good cheer, thy faith hath made thee whole". Jesus did not refer to anything about the woman, but her faith. He did not say that her education, wealth, or even tears had made her whole, but rather faith. Genuine faith in the living God can cause a fig tree to wither. Faith, according to Jesus, moves mountains. In this particular example, her faith caused her chronic medical problem to be resolved once and for all.

Therefore I say unto you, what things soever ye desire, when ye pray, believe that ye receive them, and ye shall have them. (Mark 11:24)

God is no respecter of persons, but I believe that He is a respecter of faith. The sad problem among Christians today is that they fail to exercise faith to receive, that which is prophesied to them. For instance, once they hear a prophecy about their lives, they go to sleep in anticipation of results. Such laxity or spiritual inactivity is unsupported by scripture.

Get it straight in your mind that you need to exercise faith to receive your miracle even that which is prophesied to you.

I want to relate to you another dramatic incident demonstrating the power of overcoming faith. The Bible records the story of four friends in Mark 2:2-5 who brought their fifth friend, a paralyzed man to be healed by Jesus.

As usual, a large gathering in the house made it difficult for them to enter. Yet, the four loyal friends stood together in faith for the healing of the paralytic colleague. Thank God always for friends who have faith to stand with you and believe God for all your needs.

They did not carry him to a native doctor, a fetish priest or some so-called religious clown on the backside of town. Instead, the four friends agreed in a commendable display of unity of faith to bring their sick friend to Jesus. They realized that He was in the world as the solution to all human needs. The four friends had faith, and the sick man, too, had faith. Otherwise, he would have opposed their earnest endeavors. Faith will always find a way. Faith does not take no for an answer.

In Mark 2:4, we discover an unusual and strange action:

And when they could not come nigh unto him for the press, they uncovered the roof where he was; and when they had broken it up, they let down the bed wherein the sick of the palsy lay.

Friend, this is a verse, which has always stirred me up ever since I first read it. What mighty faith this is! Some Christians give up after one or two attempts. In Matthew 7:7 the Bible commands us to "...ask, and it shall be given you; seek, and ye shall find; knock, and it shall be opened unto you". I believe that the story you just read is more than a one-time asking, seeking or knocking. Evident in that scripture is a call to persistence. Faith persists!

Returning to Mark 2:5, the account mentions that when Jesus saw their faith, he said unto the sick of the palsy, "Son, thy sins be forgiven thee." In verse 11, Jesus rewards his faith "I say unto thee, Arise, and take up thy bed, and go thy way into thee. Arise, and take up thy bed, and go thy way into thine house."

God does not want to see your fear, doubt and unbelief. Jesus did not notice people's lack of education and money or their tears. Rather Jesus saw their faith. Faith is agreeing with the word of God.

If you agree with what the devil is saying, it shall come to pass. The signs and wonders of unbelief will befall you. For instance, if you dream of a ghastly motor accident, do not be afraid! When you wake up, reject it and confess that you will live according to God's word. You do not have to go round town crying. "I had a dream last night that I had a car accident. I just know I will." No!

Agree with the word of God and confess it, and you will live. That is the key to the overcoming faith. Do not be ensnared by the words of your mouth. God, at creation set in motion certain spiritual and natural laws. What you sow is what you reap (Gal 6:7).

If you have a vision or dream, build it up on the word of God and begin to confess it. Nurture the word in your spirit, nourish it by daily confession according to the scriptures, and it will come to pass. Travail through prayer and faith; your dream will not die. In the fullness of time you will see its birth, if you uphold it by a faith-filled confession.

Be mindful of what you read, with whom you associate and what you hear. These three things will alter your life for good or bad, for life or death, for accomplishment or failure, and for faith or unbelief. If you constantly associate with unbelievers, they will help destroy your faith. But the good news is that if you associate with people of faith and Bible-believing brethren, you will become a giant in faith. The Joshuas and the Calebs of our day always flock together.

Faith is mentioned 21 times in Hebrews 11, and not without a reason. All men and women who overcame the world, subdued kingdoms, ceased the mouths of roaring lions, quenched fire and wrought righteousness (Heb 11:33-39) were people of faith. That chapter is reserved for people of faith.

The lions have not changed; the fire is the same; kingdoms continue to rebel and oppose the gospel; that same old dragon, the devil is around. All these problems still confront you today. But the good news is this: you too can overcome the world by faith.

Chapter Four

A Step Beyond

E ver since I became born again, the one thing that has always impressed me about the Bible is its flawless logic. Every necessary distinction is meticulously made and maintained throughout its pages. Every basic promise is worked out to its final logical conclusion or consequence.

There is no denying that the Bible is an authentic work of the Holy Spirit. Aside from questions about the seat of final authority in religion, the Bible does have an authority from which we cannot escape. In spite of diverse theories of inspiration, the Bible is in a distinct sense God's Word; the Seed of God's Kingdom; and a main medium of God's power.

D. L. Moody, a great American evangelist, was once asked whether he considered the Bible to be inspired. His answer was brief and to the point: "I know the Bible is inspired," he said, "because it inspires me!"

As a minister of the Gospel, I have come to put implicit and unquestioning faith in God and His Word. Let us digress for a while as I share with you valuable Scripture passages that have led me to depend tenaciously on Christ and

His Word. Because Christ identified Himself with us so completely every believer now stands in a new position to receive God's blessings:

- When Christ was crucified, we were crucified with Him. (Rom 6:6)
- When He died, we died. (Rom 6:2-3,6; Col 3:3; Gal 2:20)
- When He was buried, we were buried. (Rom 6:4-5)
- When He overcame Satan, we overcame Satan. (Col 2:15)
- When He was quickened in a new creation, we were quickened with Him. (Eph 2:5)
- When He arose from the grave, we rose with Him into newness of life. (Rom. 6:4-5; 2 Cor. 5:15; Col. 2:12; 3:1)
- When He ascended into heaven, we ascended with Him into heaven. (Eph. 2:6)
- When He sat down at the right hand of majesty on high, we sat down with Him in heavenly places. (Eph 1:18-23; 2:6)

Christ our Lord didn't die to save Himself from sin as He was sinless; neither did He need to overcome Satan's power for Himself because Satan has always been under Him. Rather, He did it all to give us authority over Satan and the joy of walking in a new creation with Him.

The Pauline revelation presents staggering proof to support the new position that believers have in Christ. Some folks would have us believe that in this life we do not have any clear promise of blessing, success or prosperity. The Scripture says we have! And I confide to you that I stand by God's word above anything else. In the Old and the New Testaments, God leaves no one in doubt concerning the blessing and success laid up for His children (3 John 2).

Look closely at Deuteronomy 29:9, "Keep therefore the words of this covenant and do them that ye may prosper in all that ye do." God is saying that if you keep or adhere to the Word, your prosperity is guaranteed. How do you keep the word? In your heart, of course!

Paul in his letter to the Church at Philippi declared, "But my God shall supply all your need according to his riches in glory by Christ Jesus," (Phil. 4:19). "All" means He will supply you what you need—spiritually, emotionally and physically—not necessarily what you want, although He can give you extra blessings if He sees fit..

The Bible is spilling over with countless promises of blessings, assurances of success in all human endeavors, and divine backing in all affairs concerning His children. But if Christians are destined for success according to God's word, why are many apparently not succeeding in the ministry, business, marriage or life?

STEP OUT

Today, I can confidently say God is looking for men and women who will believe Him. The reason is simple. It is the Bible's way to success. "Wait Bishop Nick, how can you prove that?" Someone might wonder. Here is a biblical proof. The children of Israel represent a type of the Church in their calling and commandment. God specifically called them out of bondage in Egypt and promised them a land flowing with milk and honey. (See Exodus 3:8.)

God does not call you to make mincemeat out of your life. He is a God of promotion. The land flowing with milk and honey, which God spoke of, was the Promised Land. God said He had given it to the children of Israel. After preparatory survey, they discovered to their dismay that there were giants in the land. Majority of the Israelites were shocked beyond recovery. "God has deceived us," some might have screamed in anger.

Not too long ago I studied this particular passage about the Israelites and the possession of the Promised Land. God stirred me up one night and whispered into my spirit. "My son, Nick," He said, "remember this day that all my Promised Lands have giants but, that notwithstanding, I have given the land to you for possession."

Friend, these words introduced me to a new appreciation of how to walk in faith and succeed. Living by faith is not for the fearful, weak-kneed or faint-hearted.

The Israelites did not know that—giants or no giants—God had given them the land. Giants in the Promised Land are for Christians (believers) who can share a testimony in the Promised Land when they enter in triumph and victory.

It might startle you to hear that if God gave me a Promised Land without giants, I would not take it. I love to testify to His Glory. The crisis of faith with the Israelites is similar to the woeful dilemma of many Christians today. They cannot believe God enough.

Maybe you have been in your present position of employment for too long. God desires that you go forward. He has made you the head and not the tail. Maybe you have pegged yourself to a certain amount of giving to God's work. God is saying to you. "Move up, there is a step beyond."

I want to talk about your prayer life. Occasionally I hear "Oh, Pastor Nick, in those days when I was converted I could pray for three hours non-stop." For many reasons the fire has now died out to flickering embers. Stir up the fire again! God wants more of you than your thirty minutes of dozing, religious prayer. There is a step beyond!

It could be that your once buoyant business has hit an all-time low. It is not God's will for you to suffer constant losses and to undergo frequent changes in fortune. We know who is responsible; it is the old dragon--the devil. It is time to stand upon God's word and step out in faith. God is going to be glorified in your business by your demonstration of faith. I say to you today: Believe God and His Word; there is a step beyond your present circumstances.

THEN CAME JESUS

In Luke 5:4, the Bible gives an interesting account of an event in the life of Peter, a disciple of Jesus Christ. A fisherman by profession, he went fishing all night and caught nothing. All hope was lost. He and his colleagues began to put their equipment and fishing gear together for the homeward journey. THEN CAME JESUS!

His arrival was in itself a miracle. Jesus set out to bless Peter, but He needed Peter's assistance. It was as though the Lord had asked Peter. "What can you offer to assist in spreading the gospel?" Thoughts of failure raced through Peter's mind. In shame he muttered slowly, "I am a failure, Lord, I have nothing to offer and my business is almost collapsed."

Jesus thought differently. There was something Peter had that could be of immense use – his canoe of course. "Can I climb into your canoe and preach the gospel to the multitudes?" He asked. Peter in all gladness offered the canoe. After preaching to the crowd, Jesus paid Peter for the seed he was able to sow with his empty canoe.

The logic behind the story is simple and it applies to all Christians. In order to receive God's blessings you have to make a sacrifice. You must give to receive. In Luke 5:4 the Bible records, "Now when he had left speaking, he said unto Simon, Launch out into the deep and let down your nets for a draught." This was a miracle that would ensure Peter a great harvest.

Peter's outspoken nature got the better of him in verse 5 when he said, "Master we have toiled all the night and have taken nothing."

Beloved friend, have you also toiled all day and yet received nothing? Have you worked all week without any apparent result? Have you worked all month without any success? Do not give up; you are on the brink of a miracle. Even in your impoverished condition God still needs something from you in order to bless you. God wants to see your faith, for faith makes a way where there is no way. Your life becomes new, purposeful and useful once you surrender it to God in Christ Jesus.

Jesus instructed Peter to launch out into the deep. One can gather from the statement that before the arrival of Jesus, Peter was fishing in shallow water. Similarly, today is your hour of salvation. Put all your faith in Jesus.

A few instructive points of their dialogue deserve proper regard. In verse, Peter said, "Nevertheless at thy word I will let down the net." What do you think Peter did? For the miracle or success he expected, Peter practiced the word. Peter did not just meditate upon the word; he acted it out in faith.

A key step toward realizing the success God has promised you is instant obedience to the voice of Christ.

Peter was an authority on fishing with many years' experience behind him. His authoritative experience should have been a hindrance to accepting the words of Jesus. But there is no record that it was.

The second salient point is this. Fishermen do not traditionally fish during the day except when they go deep-sea fishing. Peter, an veteran and avid fisherman, knew that fish are harder to catch during the day. He might have told Jesus something like this: "Please, Jesus, for Your information it is already daybreak, and we do not go fishing during the day."

When God wants to perform a miracle, He breaks all human formulas and rules. Because Peter chose to ignore what he knew and obey Jesus, Peter caught more than enough fish.

In your prayer life, launch out into the deep Jesus says to you. Take a step forward, wait upon the Lord in fasting and prayer, and God will move in your affairs. The deep is where the miracles are. Your healing, prosperity and abundance lie in the deep.

What we find in Luke 5:6-7a should amaze you. It says, "And when they had this done, they inclosed a great multitude of fishes; and their net brake. And they beckoned unto their partners, which were in the other ship, that they should come and help them." Thank God for Peter's obedience. His obedience yielded very fruitful results; he caught more than he ever had since becoming a fisherman.

Put the word of God first in your life. Be word-conscious! If you are going to be successful as a Christian, then learn how to be guided by God's Word.

"Be ye doers of the word and not hearers only ... for if any be a hearer of the word, and not a doer, he is like unto a man beholding his natural face in a glass" (James 1:22-23).

Don't miss the message of Luke 5:7. Peter's colleagues were stunned beyond words. The nets were so heavy, that he could not lift the net out by himself; he had to call for external help.

When God allows you to prosper, He does so that you can bless others.

In this timely book you have seen the revelation behind the mystery of salvation. You have also read about God's "Emancipation Proclamation." It is God's declaration of your total freedom. Now, having digested the principles of overcoming faith, you will begin to bear fruit in your life. You have realized that God through Christ has destined you to take a step beyond. What good news! It is the truth in Christ that sets a man free. (See John 8:32.) The WORD of God is the WILL of God. Read the will every day.

Chapter Five

Success Mindedness

Whatsoever ye do in word or deed, do all in the name of the Lord Jesus. (Colossians 3:17)

This book of the law shall not depart out of thy mouth; but thou shalt meditate therein day and night that thou mayest observe to do according to all that is written therein: for then thou shalt make thy way prosperous, and then thou shalt have good success. (Joshua 1:8)

My son, attend to my words: incline thine ear unto my sayings; let them not depart from thine eyes; keep them in the midst of thine heart; for they are life unto those that find them, and health to all their flesh. Keep thy heart with all diligence; for out of it are the issues of life. (Proverbs 4:20-23)

God wants your life to be full of success, but only as long as it is based upon His word. The reason is that when you prosper through His word, you are definitely prospering in a way that will yield eternal value in you.

The verse we read in Proverbs 4:20-23 should be central in your heart. It says, "Attend to my words." How do you attend to God's word? The phrase means "pay attention" to the instructions that I have given you. This calls for a conscious effort to read, meditate on and obey the Word.

You know too well that failure to pay attention to duties in your office for weeks without permission could earn you a dismissal. Certainly, you are mindful not to miss three consecutive meetings of your professional organization, otherwise, your name could be struck from the books.

Let me pose the question. How often do you read God's Word? Once in a while? Or when you feel like taking a glance? When you sit in church? At your convenient times? Or when some crisis comes your way? It doesn't have to be that way!

Remember the Word of God is a tree of life that produces riches, honor, promotion and joy. Therefore, attend diligently to God's Word with the same zeal you give to office duties and professional matters.

Let us take a look at Proverbs 4:21 again. It says, do not let thee word of God "...depart from thine eyes". The word of God is spiritual motivation for the human spirit. As you read God's word, yield to it, and meditate upon it day and night, it will doubtless build an image within you of your goals whether they are physical, spiritual or financial.

BUILDING A WORD LIFE

Many years ago I desired to prosper and succeed in life. Yet, I did not know God's word, His acts or His ways. I set out to go the way of the world. I did all there was to do by the system of the world. I did not know what the Bible said. I knew many who were gambling to succeed. I tried it, and it came to sorrow. I could count scores who stowed away in ships to Europe to irk out a living. I made such moves and was repatriated.

Friends said to me. "Nick, the new thing is drugs, it is a fast life and you can make it big in no time." What else could I do? I believed my friends and ended up burning off some of my fingers in one of our evil escapades.

In those days I could think of many people who seemed to think that it was possible to live by worldly standards and still be a true Christian. When I found Christ, or better still, when He found me, I discovered from God's word through His prophet Hosea, "My people are destroyed for lack of knowledge," (4:6a). God's people are destroyed by the lack of knowledge that godly men and women can and will prosper and succeed as they become diligent in God's system.

The Scripture says in 3 John 2, "Beloved, I wish above all things that thou mayest prosper and be in health, even as thy soul prospereth."

I can't convince you otherwise if you think that God does not want you to prosper or succeed. At best, I can counsel you to renew your mind with God's word in its full revelation. The biggest headaches I have had as a member of the body of Christ have arisen from the idea that you can't serve God and prosper. This garbage was sold to religious folks through the centuries, and it has been one tough lie to eradicate.

Every now and then someone will ask me: "Please can I have a word with you?" Then they will say to me solemnly as we take a seat, "Man of God, please let us be careful about this prosperity and success teaching."
"What is your reason, Sir?" is my reply.

"Eh, when people succeed and prosper, Pastor, they would not be humble again," he replies.

Often I have enlightened them: "You cannot support your thoughts with God's word."

There have been times when I wondered. "Certainly, if these principles of faith and success were true, someone would have taught them in the church." Not long ago, some churches accused me when I shared these truths about God's plan to bless us. Thank God that today many of them have found the truth at last.

When I started working with these simple principles in the Christian Action Faith Ministries, things started changing for the better. I appreciate that results don't come suddenly, but gradually. Our church is into the full revelation of God's success plan. Take a look at 2 Timothy 3:16-17,

All scripture is given by the inspiration of God, and is profitable for doctrine, for reproof, for correction, for instruction in righteousness: that the man of God may be perfect, thoroughly furnished unto all good works.

Note that it says, all scripture is given by God and is profitable for us. Instruction in God's word will definitely and purposefully change our preconceived ideas and bring us to a better understanding of GOD'S SUCCESS PLAN.

THINGS TO MEDITATE ON

In Joshua 1:8 we come across an unusual scripture verse: "This book of the law shall not depart out of thy mouth but thou shalt meditate therein day and night, that thou mayest observe to do according to all that is written therein: for then thou shalt make thy way prosperous, and then thou shalt have GOOD SUCCESS."

Several times in Joshua chapter one, we find God speaking to His servant about being courageous enough to continue the task his predecessor Moses had begun. However, Joshua 1:8 presents us with new truths. Many Christians have not read, refused to accept or simply ignored them. This is one particular verse, which has richly influenced my Christian experience. It has brought me great joy and success as I have studied and meditated on the truth in what God was telling Joshua.

This is a pronouncement of God Himself, so let us be careful as we unravel it. It is a foundation for success. We may get more out of the verse if we break it up into simpler portions. "This book of the law shall not depart out of thy mouth". The book of the law means the scriptures, or what we know today as the Holy Bible. God says His word should not depart from your mouth. Read it over and over again. This is a commandment, not just to Joshua, but also to all who desire to walk with God and know His ways. Will you accept it as your own commandment too? The law or the word of God can depart from your mouth if you allow it to.

If you allow the word to depart out of your mouth, something else apart from God's word will come out from your mouth. Can you guess what will come out of your mouth? You will end up speaking about religious mentalities, intellectual theories, latest discoveries, ways of the world, fears or other symptoms of plain unbelief.

The next portion to look at says, "...but thou shalt meditate therein day and night." Let me ask you, "What should you meditate on day and night?" The fact is that, what you meditate on day and night will eventually show in your life. It will be manifested in your words and reflected in your actions.

What does God want you to meditate on day and night? It is just what He told Joshua. "This book of the law..." Let us take a word of caution here. The Bible says in another place, "Out of the abundance of the heart the mouth speaketh" (Luke 6:45). Whether you like it or not, what is in your heart will come out when you speak. Thus, we should meditate on His Word. It should be the controlling force of our thoughts.

Friend, we must not deceive ourselves. We must make a deliberate effort to meditate on the word of God day and night. The cares of this world and the pressures of life and ministry can choke out the desire for the word of God.

The twenty-first-century Christian has a lot of forces to contend with if he is to stay true to the word of God and be able to meditate on it successfully. God's talk with Joshua (1:8) occurred several thousands of years ago, at a time when society was far different from what it is today. Joshua did not face the pressures of television, radio, billboards and advertisements that are constantly trying to get our attention. The twenty-first-century Christian has little time. As a result, he must redeem the time that he has.

With all the negative influences and time-stealing pressures today, we have other means to meditate on the Word of God day and night. We have the modern conveniences of the cassette tape recorder; CD players; Christian; and the never-ending stream of teaching seminars and fellowships among other things. Unlike Joshua, we can enjoy the Bible on audiotape even while we jog, lie in bed, drive or board an airplane for hours.

You see, the problem is simply that many don't desire to use these technological advancements to their advantage.

"But Bishop Nick, I am so busy, I don't have time," some will apologetically say.

It is simply a matter of wisdom in the use of time. I do not know what you are involved in, but I am also a very busy man.

"Oh Pastor, but you are a busy man of God," some will cry out. Of course, I am, but you must never get so busy as to miss out on meditations of the Word of God.

"So what do I do, Bishop?"

Let me offer you useful, fruitful and proven suggestions to help you in a hectic generation.

Apportion time every day to read the Bible. Be faithful at it, no matter what happens. Friends and visitors will show up at that hour, but plan in your heart to be faithful at it. I call this discipline. No man or woman has ever succeeded without personal discipline. If you can afford it, get yourself a Bible on audiocassette and play it in-between meals, when you are relaxing and at bedtime. Even if you can't afford it, go down to your local library and borrow it for free! There is no excuse!

Do you have a car? Don't just sit in the traffic looking at the latest mini-skirts and punkish haircuts. Use your cassette or CD player to meditate on the Word of God. Save some money and buy yourself a compact-style tape recorder, and take it with you to the office or as you travel by road or by air.

I am not saying that you should use your official time listening to the Word of God. What I mean is, use your break time listening to or reading the Bible or some good Christian books.

There is an important point I must emphasize here. You will find out that what you meditate on is exactly what bears fruit in your life. Take time to read and listen to other messages on healing, prosperity, holiness, evangelism, consecration and giving among others so that your Christian life will be a balanced one.

Now, for my last word on meditating on the Word of God; remember that the Bible states in Romans 10:17, "So faith cometh by hearing and hearing by the word of God."

The implication of what the apostle Paul said is that you must hear, and keep on hearing consistently if you expect your faith to grow. It says "faith cometh." If you do the hearing just once, faith for success will not come. Stay in there and hear it repeatedly until it moves you from mere mental assent to your heart.

Our next portion of scripture from Joshua 1:8 is, "...that thou mayest observe to do according to all that is written therein..." You can't give what you don't have, and you can't say what you don't know. To try either would amount to self-deception.

It is worthy to note that James 1:2 says, "Be ye doers of the word, and not hearers only." As you begin to meditate on the Word of God, your actions will begin to reflect that faith. . If your are to prosper by God's way, then it stands to reason that you must do so according to His word. When we use the word of God as your foundation you will find that there will be great consistency in life and nature. The word of God will produce success in your life.

For clear application of what l mean read Luke 6:43-49. So you may ask, "Bishop Nick, do you mean that if the word does not depart from my mouth, and l meditate on it day and night, and observe to do all that is written in the Bible, l will SUCCEED?" My plain answer is, "Yes, you will succeed! You will succeed in your marriage, job, business and education if you will do God's word."

With all due respect, allow me to ask you a question. "Does God actually intend to do all He has said in His word?" Of course, He does! Why on earth would God encourage you as His child to be a success if He is a failure? That would be strange!

Are you scared of success? You don't have to be if you know that you are a child of God, created in His image.

How do I convince you of this important point? The verse we are looking at says, "... that thou observe to do according to all that is written therein..." Simply put, God is telling you, "Be sure to do as I have said."

The next logical question is whether God would want to force you to do anything of which He has no idea. That would be unfair; but God is fair.

A dear friend of mine, Rev. Casey Treat, a pastor of a large congregation in the United States said in response to such people. "In all truth, God is the most successful Being in the universe. He's the only One who's never had to cut back, lay people off, take out a loan or lease, and has never rented anything. God is successful."

Rev. Treat, based in the Pacific Northwest of the United States of America and founder of Dominion University, emphasized that: "God teaches the principles of success to His people. Those who truly walk with God succeed. Whether it is in the financial realm or in their ministry of teaching, or sewing, those who truly walk with God can and will succeed if they use God's Principles."

This is the cardinal reason why God says, "Observe to do according to all that is written therein." That is the only way you may be able to success in God's way.

Read again from the Book of Joshua, chapter 1, verse 8, "...for then thou shalt make thy way prosperous and then thou shalt have good success." In other words, the prosperity and good success, which God desired for Joshua was dependent upon Joshua doing certain things. But this is a conditional sentence. To fully comprehend the impact of this portion of scripture, you must know what God said in the first half.

Joshua was not to allow the word of God to depart out of his mouth; he also had to meditate on the word day and night; and ensure to do exactly what was stated in the word. God implied that if Joshua would do these three things, success and prosperity would be guaranteed.

In order for you to succeed and prosper, then you need to follow the same steps that God gave to Joshua.

But before proceeding, be forewarned. Many young men and women today walk with and minister to men of God and think that that alone will bring success. This process is important and has its place in God's calling. But that alone will never bring complete success to your life. Others take off immediately after a man of God lays hands on them. They assume that laying on of hands is all that it takes.

My friend, there is more to it than this. Impartation of the spirit and the power and anointing is important, but always remember God's word to Joshua in 1:8.

Joshua's success went beyond serving Moses or receiving spiritual impartation from him. Joshua's succeeded because he did all of that and believed God's Word. We see a proof of this faith in God's word during the battle against Jericho, which resulted in the walls falling down. The feat reveals a man who knew how to believe God and meditated day and night on His word.

Can you recollect the man in the Bible who spoke words of faith to stop the sun while he fought his enemies? That was Joshua! (Joshua 10:14) In fact Joshua was a success as a soldier, statesman and captain of God's people for only one reason. He lived by the words found in Joshua 1:8.

THING TO ALWAYS REMEMBER

- Don't let God's word ever depart from your mouth.
- Meditate on God's word day and night.
- Observe to do what God has said. Follow His principles for success.
- Your own success depends on your obedience to God's Word.

Chapter Six

Foundations For Success

No human being will really be successful in the affairs of this life unless he applies the sayings of Jesus. That is, he must put the Lord's words into action. Jesus said in Luke 6:47-49

Whosoever cometh to me, and heareth my sayings, and doeth them, I will shew you to whom he is like: He is like a man which built an house, and dug deep, and laid the foundation on a rock; and when the flood arose, the stream beat vehemently upon that house, and could not shake it; for it was founded upon a rock. But he that heareth and doeth not, is like a man that without a foundation built a house upon the earth; against which the stream did beat vehemently, and immediately it fell; and the ruin of that house was great.

Some people think Jesus was referring to house construction, but that's not the case here. Remember, He was telling a parable or giving an illustration. In this short passage of scripture lies an important secret to success in life. Once we do the things Jesus says, we will have a firm foundation laid on a rock. The Bible tells us in 1 Corinthians 10:4 "...That Rock was Christ."

Over the years, I have built within my spirit a strong consciousness of success. It has not been easy reaching this level of faith and growth, but it has been worth the diligence. Gradually I have become intolerant of defeat and failure.

Do I face adversities and challenges? My answer is simple. I have gone through severe crises that would easily cause a person to even commit suicide. In fact, I have opportunities by the minute and hour to withdraw and succumb, but I refuse to. In fact, as I work right now on this revised edition of this book, I have survived the most potentially devastating crisis that a man can face. But I did not take defeat for an answer! Why? Because my life is built on the Rock of ages!

Could we do a little Bible study on these beautiful words of Jesus in Luke 6:47-49? In verses 48 and 49 we discover two builders. Both of the men mentioned in this parable are builders, for to live means to build. Every ambition a man cherishes, every deed he performs is, as it were, a building block. Gradually the structure of his life rises. Not all builders are the same, however, some are sensible, some foolish.

Furthermore, Jesus said that the man who hears His teachings and puts them to practice "is like a man which built an house, and digged deep, and laid the foundation on a rock" - Luke 6:48. This is no tent-pitching affair.

Ours is an "instant-gratification" generation, so to speak: we depend on instant tea, instant pictures, fast foods, microwaves and so on. In John White's article on "The Doorway to Holiness," which appeared in the Winter 1990 issue of Equipping the Saints Magazine.. He notes that, "We live in a day in which to become a Christian you are supposed to believe the correct beliefs. Gradually you learn the Christian jargon and gain confidence in socializing in the Christian community. This is quick fix form of Christianity which tends to produce either reformed sinners or else weak Christians."

John White is talking about the man "who without a foundation built a house upon the earth...(Luke 6:49). Such a person will later turn round and accuse everyone that the word of God does not work. But the Word works!

He who is wise makes Christ the foundation of everything he does – his education, marriage, vacation, friends and ministry.

In the second aspect of Jesus' parable we arrive at a spectacular truth, which many have missed. It has to do with the test to which the house is subjected as portrayed in verse 49 "The flood arose, the stream beat vehemently upon that house, and could not shake it: for it was founded upon a rock" –(Luke 6:48).

Get it straight–this was no minor rainstorm. Even poorly constructed houses are able to weather little storms. But the real test comes when severe storm hits. That is the time when refuge and security are needed. The house that was firmly built stood the severe test of floodwaters. It was immovable and steadfast! As we can see from the parable the secret was not in the construction of the house itself. Rather, the source of strength was the "rock" upon which the house was founded (Luke 6:48).

In this chapter, we are dealing with the foundations of success. God has shown us repeatedly that the reason many Christians do not succeed is because of a poor foundation.

There are many blockades to success. Divorce is the obstacle that will stop some men and women from achieving their goals. For some it is sickness. For a good many others, the problem may be poverty, or lack of some kind.

For everyone on earth the storms of life come and go. Like it or not, there is no escaping them. But I do know that if your life is built on Christ and you do His Words, you will rise above your limitations.

THE SOLID FOUNDATION

It is hard work to lay a good foundation. We can all agree on that. A builder must take time to check the building site. He must do some excavation and sometimes drive pilings deep into the earth. But a careless builder might decide that since a foundation is not exposed to view, it would be unprofitable to spend much time and effort on it. Actually, the reverse is the case.

For us, floods could come in the form of inflation, sudden sickness or any of the other problems you experience. But if you plant the incorruptible seed in your heart and do faithfully the things Jesus said, you WILL SUCCEED despite them. The man who builds his house on his confession only will be washed away.

Who will stand the storm? Who will stem the tide? Who will SUCCEED in the face of odds? The doer of the word will do all these things.

Our church is not just called Christian Action Faith Ministries for the fun of it. By God's grace, I have led the people through Christian action! We have acted on God's Word.

There have been times when we were pressed to the wall and surrounded by fear, but thank God we faced the storm and walked on in faith. Men of wicked imaginations have sat in judgment over my ministry and me. They have pronounced a death sentence upon God's work, but in every case we have survived by the grace of God to give our testimony today. At times, my life was even in danger. It was like standing on a precipice. One could not tell whether day would ever come and where one could be. What do you do in times like that? I look beyond my immediate attacks and fears and I refused to be stopped.

As l discovered years ago, there is a great lesson here concerning the building of solid foundations for success in any field of life. In Nehemiah 6:1 – 4, we read:

Now it came to pass, when Sanballat and Tobiah, and Geshem the Arabian, and the rest of our enemies, heard that I had built the wall, and that there was no breach left therein: (though at that time I had not set up the doors upon the gate): That Sanballat and Geshem sent unto me, saying, Come let us meet together in some one of the villages in the plain of Ono. And I sent messengers unto them saying I am doing a GREAT WORK, so I cannot come down: why should the work cease, whilst I leave it and come down to you? Yet they sent unto me four times after this sort; and l answered them after the same manner."

This is a passage full of lessons for every Christian aspiring for success. In verse 1 we learn that the enemies of Nehemiah were stirred up from sleep when they found out his exploits.

Where were Sanballat, Tobiah and Geshem when Nehemiah was serving as cupbearer to King Artaxerxes? They took no interest in Nehemiah as long as he served as an unknown cupbearer in a foreign court. Evidently, the crisis point came when Nehemiah decided to obey the Word or strive for success and come out of obscurity.

61

In chapter 2, verse 10, we learn that "When Sanballat the Horonite, and Tobiah the servant, the Ammonite heard of it, it grieved them exceedingly that there come a man to seek the welfare of the children of Israel".

The enemies were only grieved at Nehemiah's efforts. They probably only wished somehow Nehemiah would come to failure.

Understand child of God, many people will be uncomfortable about your plans for success. But I encourage you to stay on course and not be deterred.

Further on in Nehemiah 2:19 we find out, "But when Sanballat the Horonite and Tobiah the servant, the Ammonite and Geshem the Arabian heard it, they laughed us to scorn and despised us, and said, What is this thing that ye do, will ye rebel against the King?"

A new dimension crept into the enemy's strategy against Nehemiah as he forged ahead to success in what God had told him to do. Previously, in Nehemiah 2:10, they were only grieved in their hearts. But their hatred deepened. They laughed at, scorned and came to despise him and his colleagues. According to them, Nehemiah's building project was an absolute rebellion against the king. Not able to battle Nehemiah alone, they tried to make him look like a criminal in order to stop him from succeeding.

Does all this sound like a dilemma you have faced before in business, education or ministry? As you aspire for success, get it settled in your heart that hundreds may despise you and even laugh at you scornfully. What will you do? Pack it in and call it quits? Or go on in the face of accusation and threats? My word to you is 'GO ON." Child of God, don't look back. Go on and become what God has said you will be.

CALL FOR COURAGE AND BOLDNESS

I now know from two authorities, God's word and the experiences of life, that no man or woman can succeed or prosper who lacks courage, boldness and wisdom. There will be times when the flesh simply wants to cower and lie down in defeat. But you must fight it out in the spirit, where the real fight of faith is settled (Phil 3:14).

Have you closely followed the story of Nehemiah? In chapter 4 verse 1, it declares, "But it came to pass that when Sanballat heard that we built the wall, HE WAS WROTH, and took indignations, and mocked the Jews." In verse 2, they labeled Nehemiah and his colleagues. "Feeble Jews". Yes, enemies will call names, but don't be deterred. Go on to success. In verse 3, the detractors stated, "Even that which they build, if a fox go up, he shall even break down their stone wall." Is it true that foxes climb city walls? Was it also true that Nehemiah was doing such a sloppy job of no lasting effect in Jerusalem? Hardly, all the talk about foxes climbing and pulling down Nehemiah's work was inspired by jealousy.

If you have your eyes set on success, what will you do with all the jealousy that will come against you? You will not have to invite it. As your prosperity and success become more manifest, jealous sentiments against you will become more conspicuous.

We are coming to the peak of this confrontation. At a certain point in time, the enemies might have envisaged that Nehemiah was not the kind of man who could be stopped by scorn and empty threats.

Tobiah and his team tried scorn, indignation, threats and mockery of the Jews but to no avail (Nehemiah 2:10; 19; 4:1; 3). Then the enemies decided to intensify their onslaught. As we see in Nehemiah 4:8. "And conspired all of them together to come and to fight against Jerusalem, and to hinder it".

Mark this scripture now, and remember it and every day of your life. The enemies of Nehemiah's success planned an all-out assault with the sole aim of hindering his work. The satanic influences, which attempted to stop Nehemiah from doing the will of God in his generation, are still around today to make moves to stop your success.

But bear in mind the words of Jesus in John 4:34, "My meat is to do the will of Him that sent me and to finish his work." Make this your prayer and objective. If it worked for Jesus, it will work for you!

Finally let me show you a strange link in the experiences of Nehemiah. In Nehemiah 2:10; 4:1; 4:7, we read that Tobiah, Sanballat, and Geshem HEARD what Nehemiah was doing on different occasions. The issue, which was bothering me, is who was reporting events in Nehemiah's camp to the enemies?

Were there agents of Tobiah and company in Nehemiah' camp? Or were some friends of Nehemiah betraying him? Don't bother to get the answer! Why? Do what Nehemiah did! And what is that? Nehemiah did not bother his head about who had suddenly become a spy in his camp. Rather, he doggedly went on doing what God had told him to do.

God has graciously given us much success and prosperity in Christian Action Faith Ministries. Everything that happened to Nehemiah we have faced in our day and time.

Sometimes I wondered, "Would people have been so offended if I had used my father's buildings for a hotel or brothel?" I don't think so. If I had turned it into a "joint" for the perpetration of sin and evil and to promote promiscuity, I believe my friends would have been many. But the story is different today. Thousands of men and women from all walks of life and strata of society are getting on fire for God in Ghana. And sure enough, it is making some people uncomfortable. Sad isn't it?

In just 52 days, Nehemiah made a name for himself and brought glory to God Almighty and honor to his nation.

Do you promise to do the same today? Do you promise God that no enemy will deter you in the things He has told you to do? Do you promise God that all the scheming and machinations of Satan will actually motivate you to greater exploits?

If these are the words of your mouth according to the desire of your heart then together we can shout, "THE GOD OF HEAVEN, HE WILL BLESS US; THEREFORE WE HIS SERVANTS WILL ARISE AND BUILD." Amen, and so shall it be in Jesus' name!

Chapter Seven
Destined For Success

You have by now established in your heart that beyond a doubt God wants you to succeed in this life as a Christian. However, the Scriptures assembled below indicate that you have a crucial role to play in making your dreams of success come true. I want to show you how to do it.

I had fainted, unless l had believed to see the goodness of the Lord in the land of the living. (Psalm 27:13)

Yet a little sleep, a little slumber, a little folding of the hands to sleep: So shall thy poverty come as one that travelleth, and thy want as an armed man. (Prov. 6:10-11)

Seeth thou a man diligent in his business? He shall stand before kings; and he shall not stand before mean men. (Prov. 22:29)

Therefore l say unto you, what things soever ye desire, when ye pray believe that ye receive them, and ye shall have them. (Mark 11:24)

From this moment onward, develop your faith to the point that you don't allow negativism to come out of your mouth. Will you start believing that every word you say will come to pass?

IMAGE CHANGE

The real problem for many people is that they walk around with a negative mindset. As it were, they never seem to think "any good thing will ever come out of Nazareth."

The majority of Christians who know the word of God are bugged by laziness of the spirit. All their lives they don't grow beyond daily confessions of faith. Every day they go on a "claiming spree." Even in the Old Testament when the children of Israel cried for manna from heaven and God did not spoon-feed them. They had to go out and fetch for themselves what God had provided.

It does not matter where you come from, what your family background is, or how educated you are. You can move from poverty to prosperity, or from sickness to health, if you will first change your inner image.

"But Bishop Nick, your case is different," some will say. My friend, understand me. No man or woman in my family was born-again before my salvation. I did not have any family example that succeeded by standing irrevocably on the word of God. But that did not affect me. Not at all! Gradually, by the word of God, I laid aside all negative images, the restriction of society, and the limitations on my life.

On this point, the apostle Paul has a word for us from 1 Corinthians15: 10, "But by the grace of God I am what I am; and his grace which was bestowed upon me was not in vain; yet not l, but the grace of God which is with me."

It is obviously a dangerous position to become self-reliant and self-sufficient. This state of mind so prevalent in body of Christ often leads to frustration and disappointment in our lives. Consider that, if Paul had dwelt on his past, he would have been discouraged. But Paul said, "By the grace of God l am what I am."

The miracle of success began when I realized that I am valuable to God When I realized how much God esteems me, how He created me in His own image, as one of His offspring's, I refused to let anybody on earth make me feel inferior or unworthy.

I cherish what Mark Twain said, "Keep away from people who try to belittle your ambition. Small people always do that, but really great people make you feel that you, too, can become great."

Doesn't the Bible say that if you walk with the wise you will be wise? From now on examine your company, and keep pace with those who have a sense of destiny in their lives.

Do you have an identity crisis in your life? As a Christian many years ago I faced a similar dilemma until I read the words of Mary Cowley, a famous Dallas businesswoman. She said, "You are somebody because God never wastes His time to make a nobody."

The greatest discovery you can ever make is your true identity in God. Realize that God never planned for you to be a failure in life. Jesus did not come to condemn you. Neither do I.

The Word of God says, "God sent not His Son into the world to condemn the world; but that the world through him might be saved" –(John 3:17).

The story is told about a young Negro in South America who was told to accept his inferiority and live with it. Can you imagine his reply? He said, "How can I be inferior, when I am of God."

I agree that success cannot be achieved effortlessly. I am not selling you some 'instant formula' from a Hollywood commercial. Instead, we are sharing precious truths from the Bible, which generations have ignored. By renewing your mind with these truths, you can start on the trail to a new beginning in Christ. All sort of amazing miracles will begin in your life as you discover and accept the image of God in you and your potential in His word. The Bible reassures us, "You are God's workmanship," (Eph. 2:10).

I read a challenging passage written by famous evangelist, Dr. T. L. Osborn in his classic, You Are God's Best. His subject was: The Worth of Self-Value. He wrote:

• **SELF-VALUE** will rid you of all jealousy because you will never again want to be anyone else.

• **SELF-VALUE** will wipe out inferiority because you are in God's class of being and He, in you, is greater than any PERSON or any POWER outside of you (1 John 4:4)

• **SELF-VALUE** will eliminate fear of failure or defeat because nothing can stop you and God working together.

• **SELF-VALUE** will give you courage because you discover that with God at work in you, you become indomitable.

• **SELF-VALUE** will cause you to stand up tall, to square your shoulders, to walk with a steady stride, and to rise to the level of the importance for which God created you"

I have read these words by Dr. Osborn many times, and as a result, I have seen God's power performing all His works in me. You need to take the first step – RECOGNIZING YOUR VALUE!

Now from this moment onward, the seeds of God's greatness will germinate in you by His word. You see, whatever one can say about parent is equally true of their offspring. In the plan of God, he arranged that whatever could be said about Him could also be said about you. In Genesis 1:28, God said, "be fruitful and multiply, and replenish the earth, and subdue it, and have dominion over every living thing."

All the possessions that God gave to mankind are listed in Genesis 29-30. Trace and find out that God never planned for you or any of mankind to have sickness, fear, inferiority, defeat, or failure. God's family is supposed to represent Him and, of course, to reflect His lifestyle on earth.

You may wonder, "But man of God, what can I do about it? Let this principle take deep root in you. Begin to see and respect yourself as a member of divine royalty. God is at work in you right now!

At this point, I intend to focus on some basic aspects of how you can achieve success as a child of God and hold on to it. Interestingly, these principles will work not just in ministry but also in any realm of life, if you work at them diligently. Half-hearted commitment to objectives will never get you far. At best, all your plans will be stillborn.

VISION

A few chapters back, l was sharing with you how to bring your plans to fulfillment. You also learned that God's family is supposed to represent Him and reflect His lifestyle on earth. This portion on how to work on the vision in your heart follows in the same vein: God is not purposeless. He has a vision.

Rev. Casey Treat defined vision as, "A mental picture of a future state." I agree with him because many people who talk about vision in the body of Christ don't have a mental picture.

Someone once asked Thomas Edison how he managed to give the world so many inventions. He said, "Because I never think in words, I think in pictures." Is that what you do, too? There is no way you will succeed without envisioning in your mind the future state, which you seek to attain.

Often I have come across many adventurous young men who talked about great plans for the future. Often I enquire, "What is your vision?" They would respond, "Eh, Bishop Duncan-Williams, I am just moving faith like Abraham."

"Did the Bible say Abraham was just rambling in the wilderness?" I reply.

They respond, "God will work things out."

Many of these precious Christian folks are operating with zeal but without knowledge. God can drop a dream, goal or desire in your heart but you must receive and nurture it in your spirit.

A classic example of this is found in Habakkuk 2:2 that reads, "And the Lord answered me, and said, write the vision and make it plain upon tables; for the vision is for an appointed time, but at end it shall speak, and not lie though it tarry, wait for it because it will surely come, it will not tarry". Read again what God told Habakkuk about visions.

- What is it that you must do?
- You must know the vision!
- The vision must be part of you!
- Read and mediate about your vision daily!
- God has appointed a time for your vision!
- You must begin to work your way toward your vision!
- Have some patience for the vision to come to pass!

Remember, God told Joshua, "See, I have given into thine hand Jericho, and the King thereof, and the mighty men of valour."

Joshua was within reach of Jericho, though he was yet to capture it, God said He had already given Jericho to him. Joshua, as a leader and a man destined for success, had to begin to see that what God has said was true even before it really happened.

I am sad to say that the main reason millions of people ramble aimlessly through life, is that they have no vision. They have no motivation. And the Bible says that without a vision (a motivating force) you will perish. You cannot afford to wander in a thousand directions all your life. Are you destined for success? Create a vision for your family, business, or ministry, and go for it!

I love what Dr. Yonggi Cho said, "Don't worry about getting faith. If you have a vision, you'll get faith." Do you understand that statement? Before proceeding, I offer you the following admonition:

- You must establish a daily sense of discipline to get you to where you want to be.
- Establish optimistic goals that stretch, challenge and excite you. Then go for it!
- f a man has no goals, then it tells you something about the man. What is it?
- Failure to plan is planning to fail!
- Build a good self-image in the Word and remember: you will only attract people who are like you!
- Encourage, motivate and inspire the people around you!
- Prosperity, divine health, peace, joy and fulfillment are not optional blessings – THEY ARE RESPONSIBILI-TIES. If you are not an example of it, if you are not the Word made flesh, then others will never get it!
- Build relationships with people!

- Communicate – implant your vision in others!
- Walk by faith in God's word!
- Be willing to change when change comes!

I entrust the words of Dr Robert Schuller to you: "Your role, plus your goal, plus the toll will equal success!" Amen.

Chapter Eight
My Testimony

It is good for a man to constantly remember where he came from, especially if he is a servant of God. This practice serves several purposes. Among them, it helps one to remain humble regardless of any promotions that come in his endeavors, and it also allows for total dependence on God in all things. I believe it is for these reasons that God repeatedly reminded King David of his lowly beginnings. Before he became ruler of Israel, he was a mere shepherd boy.

And it shall come to pass, if thou shalt hearken diligently unto the voice of the LORD thy God, to observe and to do all his commandments which I command you this day, that the LORD thy God will set thee on high above all nations of the earth: And all these blessings shall come on thee, and overtake thee, if thou shalt hearken unto the voice of the LORD thy God. (Deut 28:1-2)

Keep therefore the words of the covenant, and do them, that ye may prosper in all that ye do. (Deut 29:9)

Being confident of this very thing, that he who hath begun a good work in you will perform it until the day of Jesus Christ. (Phil 1:6)

I have never failed to keep my humble beginnings in proper perspective. He took me out of the miry clay, set my feet fast upon the rock, and put a song on my mouth to sing. Beloved, I owe it all to the Lord Jesus Christ. He is the one who makes all the difference in my life.

You will read for the very first time in print, the amazing testimony of my life. Every step of the way, you will stand with me to glorify God for the spectacular deliverances, miraculous healings and the divine grace and favor He has demonstrated in my life, even before I was born. The blessings and prosperity of God in my life are no secret, and I am a living testimony to His faithfulness.

God declared of the Prophet Jeremiah, "Before I formed thee in the belly I knew thee; and before thou camest forth out of the womb I sanctified thee, and ordained thee a prophet unto the nations" - Jer 1:5

THE TRAVAILS

The story of the circumstances under which I was born is a clear indication that God overrules the schemes and designs of the enemy to accomplish His purposes. One day my mother said to me, "Nicholas, have I ever told you what travails I endured to give birth to you? In every way, I was taken aback.

Curiously, I replied, "Mama, what is it that you have not told me all these years about my birth."

"Sit down please," she said to me encouragingly, directing me to a large chair.

"I daily bless the Name of the LORD for your life and His calling you," she said. "Whenever I look back more than three decades ago and recollect it all, I see the finger of God in your life both to preserve and to use you."

My mother carefully recounted how she battled through nine months of bleeding when she conceived me. It was as if the devil made every move to destroy me before birth. But I rejoice to say the seed of the LORD can never be destroyed. Be assured also that whatever God has planted in your life, He will also watch over to preserve it for His name's sake.

When the devil realized that he could not prevent my birth, he initiated other schemes to wreck God's plan for my life. He attacked my parents and brought about a divorce. As is usually the case, the separation between my father and mother rather had adverse effects on my adolescent years.

Consequently. I was confronted with all kinds of problems at an early age. More so, because I belonged to a large family of brothers and sisters, lack of financial support stifled my education.

A primary setback was that, for several reasons, I had to be enrolled in school at a rather advanced age in comparison to my colleagues. I was a clear four years older than the oldest mate in my class. The jeers and attendant discomfort turned me into a bully. But this did not last for long. The embarrassment of my late entry to school forced my mother to make a difficult decision. We moved to Wa in the Upper Region of Ghana. The harsh realities of life and deprivation began to take their toll on me. My consolation in Wa was that a large number of my classmates were also far older than the stipulated age. It gave me some breathing space for a while.

Because of the demands of my mother's profession as a nurse we transferred to Bolgatanga after a sojourn of two years in the cruel Harmattan land.

The move to Bolgatanga did not change my situation to any degree. If anything, I had new hardships with which to contend. In fact, I spent my initial year there at home because I could not raise money to pay for my school fees.

BOLGATANGA MARKET

After a careful survey of my dilemma, I decided it was time to work to support my self. This was not an easy task.

I struck a bargain with local newspaper vendors who supplied me bulk copies of the Daily Graphic on a daily basis. Further supplies from vendors obviously depended on my integrity in making prompt returns as well as my dexterity in sales. Each morning, well before daybreak I ran through a quick bath, whistling discordantly to encourage myself. The harsh Harmattan weather blew over my load of Daily Graphic newspapers. Nevertheless, by sheer drive and determination, I soon established myself as the "Accra boy" who made incredible sales.

As soon as sales were over, I trotted home and donned my school dress. In this way I gradually put behind me the dreadful consequences of inability to support myself while in school. There is no denying that the presence of large sums of money in the hands of a schoolboy can be a negative influence on him. In fact, my newspaper sales adversely affected my classes over the months. Added to this, there was always the enticement to labor for more money to buy other personal items.

I took on one more responsibility; that of pushing locally designed wooden food carriage trucks. This generated more income for me in spite of the strain on my young body.

The truck pushing business in the Bolgatanga market was a highly competitive one. It called for all the imagination and creativity I could muster. For days I worked assiduously on my hired food carriage truck. I painted it with bright colors. With all my youthful artistry, I made awkward designs on the front and sides to attract food sellers. My efforts yielded the desired results. Customers wrestled over who should benefit from my beautifully decorated carrier. In a matter of weeks, I had established my position as a hardworking food carriage truck pusher all over the Bolgatanga market.

One day I received some discouraging news about newspaper sales business. The proprietors had gone bankrupt and wound up the business. A whole range of thoughts raced through my mind as I braced myself for the loss of income from my newspaper sales.

The owner of my truck called in a few mornings after the newspaper sales ended. "Small Nick," he said to me, with his hand gently tapping my quivering shoulders. "Eh, due to some problems I'm encountering, I have decided to withdraw the truck and move out of town."

I was momentarily dazed by the full implication of his words. As I bowed my head, heavy beads of sweat mingled with my tears of despair and dropped on the truck owner's hands. An inexplicable silence engulfed me. After a short while he said to me, "Goodbye Nick, and God help you." He walked drunkenly over to the side of our kitchen window and took hold of his truck.

I cannot recall how long I stood there watching him push away the truck, but the noise of two cocks locked up in a tumultuous combat in the corner of the room stirred me out of my stupor. Considering the day a rather gloomy one, I withdrew into bed and lay down for hours analyzing the events of my life. My mother somehow managed to raise the money to cater for my needs easing my agony over the closure of my businesses.

BACK TO ACCRA

It was time to return to Accra in 1972. I had been in Bolgatanga for five years. My mother invited me one chilly morning to her room. She stared at me and said, "Nick, I have been transferred back to Accra, and so we have to go." I sighed heavily and walked back to my room. A new feeling came over me; it was neither sadness nor joy, but it certainly was one of a welcome relief. Accra might offer better opportunities, I thought to myself.

Life and business in the capital city of Accra were certainly different from Bolgatanga. A whole range of ideas rolled through my mind, and school was no longer an interest. The reason was simple – I had outgrown it. I was no longer in a mood to tolerate the taunting and jeers of colleagues who felt that I was far too big for my class. Besides, I could not stand being a bully anymore.

I was determined to make up quickly in Accra for all that I had lost in Bolgatanga. Several times, I strolled through the teaming crowd of pedestrians, visitors, sellers and buyers. I carefully surveyed the land for a couple of weeks. Then finally I made a move.

With the small capital I was able to raise, I embarked on the business of selling "P.K." chewing gums to the afternoon cinemagoers at the Opera Square. This was brisk business, but obviously not enough to sustain me. Therefore, earlier in the morning I went over to the Accra Central train station where I helped to carry bags of foodstuffs for a fixed fee. Late in the evenings, most of the time I walked the nearly ten-kilometer distance to Kokomlemle, just to save some money. I stayed with my uncle, who, in the absence of accommodation, offered me his garage. At the crow of the cock at dawn, I crawled out of the garage and hurried to the Accra Central train station.

The new friends I made introduced me to gambling on the jackpot. This was a welcome escape from the nightly loneliness of my garage apartment. It was indeed better company than the cockroaches, which raced fiercely in the darkness of my garage apartment.

News reached me of my mother's invitation for me to meet her for some crucial discussions. She labored to explain the need for me to further my education.

"Mother, you know my peculiar problem," I explained to her. "You know that I am now too old for my class and that I cannot stand the sneers anymore." But my mother was not convinced by my explanation.

After several rounds of discussions and "official intervention," I opted to go and stay with my father, a former politician, at the Airport Residential Area. This was a decision, which marked the beginning of events that were to alter the course of my life.

My father was in a "no-nonsense" mood concerning my explanations about my inability to return to thee classroom. With one lightning-quick decision, he opted to deposit me in an elementary school in Madina, near Accra. Before long, I discovered that I had stayed too far away from the chalk, the teacher, and the classroom. Too many societal influences had firmly gripped me. The discos and blazing voices of the highlife had taken a toll on my heart. I could not concentrate on my studies. One day I walked out never to go back again. I was determined to seek laurels elsewhere.

This time the sound of the airplanes attracted me. Soon, I made a large company of friends by helping travelers check their luggage and doing other miscellaneous assignments I could find. I established myself at the airport as a self-appointed travel agent.

SENSE OF DESTINY

As the days rolled into weeks and months, I began to look at life in a different perspective. "Couldn't there be more to life than being the flotsam and jetsam of society?" I soliloquized.

Suddenly a new sense of awakening came over me. It was like stirring up out of a stupor to discover you are the child of a king, a prince without even knowing it. How can I express this feeling I had to you? It was like a veil pulled off my mind to understand suddenly that life offered new challenges. It was like receiving an injection of reality on the brink of hopelessness. If you will allow me, I would say that a new sense of destiny seized me and I could not wriggle out of it nor comprehend its meaning. Worst of all, my position as a 'goroboy' or airport attendant, did not line up with this new uncomfortable luxury of thinking.

Gradually, I began to re-examine my life. I felt within my heart somehow new vistas and new horizons lay in store for my generation and me. But how? I did not know! In the same vein, I realized that there were also some strong forces determined to destroy my life.

One evening in 1974 I walked into my father's presence as he reclined on his sofa gazing at the sunset. He took one cursory glance at me and returned his gaze at the sunset. I could figure out what he thought about me. If anything, he considered me a wayward young man – listless, hopeless, a failure waiting to happen. But certainly that was not God's opinion of me. Before I could state my purpose he fired at me. "What do you want?" I pulled myself together quickly as my thoughts ran haywire.

I stammered a reply: "Please I want to talk to you about my plans to go to America." He let out a rocking cough and retorted. "Alright, thanks for coming. I will see you later." All this while, he had not as much as stolen a second glance at me. With heaviness and uncertainty, I slammed the door behind me.

I left my father's room with resolute determination to prove him wrong. "I must pay any price to succeed in life." I swore to myself, making no secret of my vow to my street friends.

With an air of urgency and importance, I told my friends as we watched over across the Accra airport runway. "I am simply fed up with Ghana, I am tired of this land." Whether they believed my words or not did not really matter to me. Every young man I knew had made plans to go to America or Europe in search of the 'golden fleece.' As far as I knew, that was the only route to success and recognition, and I was not going to be left out of the race.

ABORTIVE STOW-AWAY

In the middle of 1974, my plans for going to Europe were cut and dried. There was no going back. Because of the dangerous nature of my line of action I thought it wise to conceal my plan from my parents and close associates. Two routes were open to me. The first possibility was to travel by air, but I readily ruled out that option because I did not have enough money to buy a plane ticket.

The next consideration was to stow-away on a foreign shipping vessel bound for Europe. This was a highly dangerous venture. There were many stories about Ghanaian boys who stowed-away on foreign shipping vessels only to be cast overboard into the sea to be mauled and killed by sharks when they were discovered by the captains.

For nights, I lay sleepless calculating the risk involved in what I was about to do. "This could mean life or death," I thought to myself, "but there is no way out for me." My mind was made up!

To avoid detection by my parents and friends, I wrapped a couple of shirts and trousers in a polythene bag and headed for the lorry station before daybreak.

"Which vehicle is going to Kumasi?" I enquired with a shivering voice. The officials pointed to a bus en-route to Abidjan. I hurriedly boarded it for the first leg of my trip to 'greener pastures'. The second leg was from Kumasi to Abidjan.

Abidjan, the capital of Ivory Coast offered me one problem: the language barrier. I did not give much attention to this because I viewed myself as a passenger in transit. By clever scheming and evasion of questions about my identity, I smuggled myself on board a ship headed for France. I squeezed myself amongst a pile of timber logs. Once again, I took stock of the items I had on me for the journey. In the midst of some long goalkeeper socks I had hidden some French bread. I had enough in my estimation to last an uncertain number of days. I had also carefully ensconced a small water container. To beat security, I had donned all my dresses–two trousers and two heavy-duty shirts and sweaters, in addition to two coats. I was set for life in the logs.

Then as often is the case, the unexpected happened. I had been in the logs for seven days and seven nights. As far as I could tell, there was no difference between the days and a night. I was completely under self-imposed restriction–seven days in lying position.

The torrential rains came down in drips and later in heavy downpour. My fortitude and courage were stretched to their limits. I was suddenly faced with the grim reality of death from cold and hunger in the midst of the logs. As the ship tossed turbulently with the cruel waves, seawater covered the logs where I was hiding. The only option open to me was to come out and surrender to the ship captain, an action that meant possible death. As I stretched and stepped out of hiding, I came face to face with other stowaways amidst the logs who had also been forced to surrender by the unexpected rain.

The captain of the ship seemed set to cast us overboard. The chief mate of the ship appeared on the scene and started asking our names.

"My name is Nicholas," I said humbly as he approached me. Suddenly the chief mate stopped in his tracks. He gazed meaninglessly into my eyes. My thoughts raced wildly at this point; it was like standing on a precipice ready to be pushed over to death. After a while he said, "My son is also called Nicholas."

I could not fit the pieces together–how his interest in my name could mean a narrow escape. He discontinued asking the names of the rest of my colleagues and walked over to the captain of the ship for further private discussions on our fate. After a lengthy argument and some angry gesticulations from the captain, the possibility of the death sentence was quashed. We were marched without further interrogation to a cargo hold beneath the ship. Despite the fact that it was dungeon without adequate light and feeding, it was unquestionably better than lying among the logs.

WAY BACK HOME

Finally, when the ship reached France and berthed at the port of Marseilles, we were graciously released with a stern warning not to disclose our identity in town. We found harbor jobs to help defray our hotel bills. But, I was in quest of deeper adventures, and that meant more money.

Before I could settle down in Marseilles, the police arrested me as they swooped on a company of rioting port workers. This time, however, the officials were bent on ensuring that I was deported to Ghana. On my homebound journey, I was put on another ship to Barcelona in Spain and then to Dakar in Senegal. The French officials there put me aboard a plane, which was destined for Accra.

Just when the aircraft touched the runway in Accra, I made up my mind to pull a fast one on my father. I could not bear to disclose to him the details of my abortive stowaway attempt and consequent deportation.

Therefore, with the little amount of foreign currency I had on me, I walked over to the Duty Free Shop and bought a giant-sized bottle of Johnnie Walker whisky and presented it to my father under the pretext that I had just flown in from the J.F. Kennedy International Airport in New York. I lied to please him.

ANOTHER MISSION IMPOSSIBLE

The days and weeks after my deportation were difficult. I was gripped with uneasiness, and I itched to go back to Europe. In 1975, I traveled by road to Abidjan where I smuggled myself once again aboard a ship destined for Haifa, Israel.

After a few days on the high seas, I surrendered to the captain with the hope that he would consider me for a job. This plan fizzled out, and I was locked up and finally brought back to Takoradi.

The rest of 1975 was devoted to working out new designs and schemes to achieve the lofty goals that were sprouting in my mind. Meanwhile, my company of friends multiplied and I spared no effort in telling them glowing stories of the charm and beauty of Europe based on my faint recollections.

THE GOD FACTOR

With uncontrollable intensity, ideas about God and the essence of creation suddenly flooded my mind. The more I fought these thoughts; fear and anxiety clouded my mind. It suddenly struck me that there must be a "God-factor" in the affairs of men and I set my heart to unravel this mystery.

I took a trip toward the end of 1975 to the Western Region of Ghana. I walked alone for several kilometers through thick tropical forest to a popular shrine in a village recommended by friends. The fetish priest welcomed me with glee, but just for a moment. He set to work to consult his gods about me. Without ceremony, the priest shot out of his inner court to the reception and stared aimlessly at me. He went into the inner court again, this time performing frenzied dancing and gaggling of a weird nature. The fetish priest came out again with a cold lifeless look in his eyes. He studiously positioned himself in front of me.

"Young man, who are you? He questioned blankly.

I stammered a reply, "Eh, I am from Accra."

He did not seem satisfied with my evasive answer. "I say tell me who you are now!"

A cold disarming fear ran through my body. With renewed boldness to cover up my apparent perplexity. I managed to say; "Please I am a young man from Accra who wants your gods to help me succeed in life."

The fetish priest shook his bald head several times and then tossed his staff. He said to me, "Young man, I cannot do anything for you."

I nearly fainted at the words of the fetish priest. By his look, he was in no mood for any questions from me. I walked out of the hamlet to embark on a long, wearisome journey back to Accra. You can imagine my state of consternation. Further visits to various "spiritual" churches did not help matters. They only stirred up more questions about life to which I could not find answers. Though not yet saved I had a deep knowledge of God's call on my life.

However my understanding of preachers based on those whom I already knew, was limited. To me, a preacher's life was that of resignation, scorn and deprivation. Almost all the ministers of the Gospel I could think of then were barely making ends meet. Simply put, many of the servants of God wore no decent clothing and portrayed a sorry picture of their position as ambassadors of the Most High God.

My father's ambassadorial position enabled me to discover what it meant to represent a country. Therefore, even in my ignorance, I could hardly reconcile the "poverty is piety" theology with God's Word that His children were the Kingdom's ambassadors (2 Cor. 5:20). The reason I decided to stay far away from God and His calling was to avoid becoming like "my preaching fore-fathers." I managed to convince myself that if God wanted to use anybody as His instrument, it certainly could not be me. But, dear friend, I did not know, nor had I ever read, the following scripture:

> *For ye see your calling, brethren, how that not many wise men after the flesh, not many mighty. Not many noble, are called: But God hath chosen the foolish things of the world to confound the wise; and God hath chosen the weak things of the wise; and God hath chosen the weak things of the world to confound the things which are mighty: And base things of the world, and things which are despised hath God chosen yea, and things which are not, to bring to naught things which are: That no flesh should glory in his presence. (1 Corinthians 1:26-29)*

I had never read this powerful piece of scripture, so I vowed to put God behind me and put the world before me. I prepared a roster and discotheque attendance schedule, which I posted atop my bed. I dutifully committed myself to have all the fun and fame life could offer. Along with my friends, I went from cinema halls to discotheques day after day. We graduated form lower degrees of sin to higher levels of iniquity.

Turning Points

Some of the evil spirits I had consulted in various places began to torment and haunt me every night. I could not sleep. I heard all kinds of weird voices, putting demands on me to commit suicide. I lost control of myself. I needed help but did not know how or where to be free.

The year 1976 will forever remain indelible on my mind. It was the year of new beginnings. One night, I could hardly sleep because of the demonic attacks. I was under great strain and stress and I suffered hallucinations. A voice commanded me to light a candle in my bedroom, so I did. The voice once again commanded me to stick my right palm upon the blazing flame of the candle. For some reason, I momentarily lost all consciousness of pain as my fingers roasted upon the candle flame. My senses were lulled. My sense of resistance was lost as I yielded completely to the evil voices.

Then suddenly, I came to myself. Sharp, painful sensations ripped through my heart. The pain was unbearable, almost excruciating. I could not believe my eyes–my three right middle fingers were burnt like mashed meat. Blood oozed out profusely from the stumps of my fingers. I shouted from my room, "Help me! Help me! I am dying," with all the energy left in my body.

Spasms of agonizing pain rocked my heart. I could not bear the pain any more. The sound of footsteps approached my door, and someone forcefully flung it ajar. I passed out.

I woke up to discover that I was firmly strapped to a bed at Ward 8 of the Korle Bu Teaching Hospital in Accra. A nurse standing by my bed held my hand and said to me. "Nick, you missed death narrowly."

TIME FOR REFLECTION

Four months in the bed of affliction offered me adequate opportunity to reflect on the whole spectrum of my wretched life. My friends, both boys and girls, were all gone. The disco with its upbeat atmosphere meant nothing to me with my heavily bandaged hand. All the questions that lay dormant in my mind re-surfaced. "What is life all about? Where does a man go after death? Is this all there is to life? Is man a pawn sold out to blind fate and forces beyond his control?" These are just a sample of the burning questions, which flooded my mind on the bed of affliction.

But one day, God closed in on me. An Indian woman by the name of Mrs. Rajj came to preach the gospel of Jesus Christ to me. She was accompanied by the Acquah sisters and some Christian nurses at Korle Bu Teaching Hospital, who boldly shared the Good News of God's saving grace and deliverance with me. As the days passed, a newfound peace flooded my soul. To my amazement, my restlessness abated. The Acquah sisters labored patiently to explain the knotty questions I raised. When I was discharged on December 23, 1976. I knew beyond any shadow of a doubt that I had become a new man in Christ Jesus. I spent hours searching the Word of God to understand the mysteries of His knowledge.

The Acquah sisters invited me to the Church of Pentecost where I graciously received the baptism in the Holy Ghost. I devoted whole days to fasting and prayers to know the will of God for my life. God was working rapidly on my behalf. I intended in my heart to be steadfast and faithful in my commitment to God and church activities. I walked several kilometers every day to attend the Church of Pentecost fellowship meetings. The miles became yards of walking distance as I sang and prayed in tongues all the way to and from church.

BIBLE SCHOOL

Zeal for the LORD came over my life. Day and night, my mind was filled with evangelism and the things of God. As I sat one evening watching a "Redemption Hour" television program in Accra, the famous Nigerian international evangelist, Rev. Dr. Benson Idahosa preached a Holy-Ghost-inspired sermon, which he concluded with an invitation to

Ghanaians who wished to be trained in a Charismatic-oriented Bible School. The Lord said immediately to my heart. "Apply and go, for I have opened a door for you."

I did, and that has forever channeled the course of my ministry. With a full scholarship from the Archbishop, I spent my days knowing that I was in the perfect will of God.

The Bible School in Benin City, Nigeria offered me a great opportunity to revive my academic faculties. Because of my inability to pursue education since I dropped out of the primary school, I had serious challenges coping with the rigorous academic work. What really sustained me was my dependence upon God in prayer, and of course, the personal encouragement accorded me by the Archbishop, who had then become my mentor. The lecturers understood my predicament and were very lenient with me. I survived the school and graduated in 1978.

BIRTH OF C.A.F.M.

Upon my return to Ghana, I went back to the Church of Pentecost, where I started fellowship after my conversion. I sought then to be engaged as an evangelist with the church. Rev James McKeown, who was then the head of the church, turned me down and advised me to try elsewhere. He explained to me the negative experiences the church had gone through with evangelist and such situations.

For some time I felt discouraged and dejected. But one thing the Church of Pentecost, and the Bible School developed in me was the zeal for prayer. Studying under the Archbishop meant that you did not give up on things like this. He succeeded in infusing into my very being, some inner tenacity and resilience. So I was determined to work for God in spite of the apparent setback.

I consulted with a few senior ministers like Brother Enoch encouraged me to Agbozo, the head of Ghana Evangelical Society, and Rev Mensah of the Full Gospel Church, who both pursue what God had laid on my heart to do.

I began to organize Saturday prayer meetings in my father's house at the Airport Residential area. Along the line, the Archbishop sent Rev J. S. B. Coker to assist me in the work I was doing. After some months of increased growth, I started Sunday services at the Association School. With this, some people left the group because they belonged to their own churches.

The church, which I later called, Christian Action Faith Ministries, began to grow. We moved from the Association School to the Student's Hostel, then back to my father's residence, and then to the Teachers' Hall, and back again to my father's residence. From there we experienced some sturdy growth, and so we moved to the Trade Fair site, and finally to our present location at the Spintex Road.

My ministry attracted many young people from the schools and colleges, as well as adult from the mainline churches because of the visible miracles, healings, and great teachings on Faith and Prosperity. Today, many of these young people have also pioneered churches, and General Overseers, with some already ordained as bishops. By God's grace, my influence has gone far, both nationally and internationally.

One chronicler of Church History in Ghana, Susan Hanson, sums it all up in her book, A Nation Touched By The Fire of Heaven:

> Today, the Christian Action Faith Ministries has churches in almost every continent of the world. He is also the Presiding Bishop and General Overseer. The

"mega" church at its headquarters, attracts crowds close to 5,000 and above in a typical Sunday service. Many lives have been transformed, given purpose and direction, and God has used Rev Duncan-Williams in several miracles, healings, and signs. He has seen the power of God move in diverse ways. He also wields much influence in governmental circles. Affectionately called the 'The People's Bishop', one can confidently say that Bishop Duncan-Williams is one Neo-Pentecostal minister who literally 'junkets' the whole world with the gospel message, holding several meetings outside the shores of this country.

To God be the glory!

Chapter Nine
God's Man Must Succeed

At this point, I am going to make some dramatic and challenging observations. They may seem so different from your present beliefs that you may question whether or not they are really biblical.

The fact that you have not seen something before is no indication that it does not exist. Also, the fact that you have not heard it before does not make it untrue.

Many people–and they are on every continent–believe that poverty and prosperity are both matters of birth and luck, that they are reserved for certain classes of society. But they say that some people are meant to be poor and others meant to be rich. Friend! that is certainly not what the Word of God says.

Dr. John Avanzini, President of "His Image Ministries" (HIM) and an acclaimed authority on Biblical Economics, has said, "God did not predetermine who would be rich and who would be poor. He simply created His spiritual laws and freely gave them to everyone. Every person then has a choice–to implement the laws of poverty, or to implement

God's spiritual laws of prosperity." Ministers of the gospel are not exempted from God's prosperity plan.

The unfortunate 'poverty is piety' concept has been with us for centuries. The Devil has sold it out from nation to nation that Christians have accepted it without testing it against the scriptures.

Since God raised me in the late 70s, I have labored in the gospel of Jesus Christ, preaching, teaching and healing. I have ministered to tens of thousands of people in my generation in great crusades and in local church fellowships. My whole life is committed to God's calling to bring revelation and salvation through His Son Jesus Christ, to the world.

It has been tough and rough, my friend. To tell you the truth, there were times when I did not know what the next day had in store for my family and me. I have seen want! I have known deprivation! I have tasted poverty at the dredges! But you may be interested to know that I did not surrender to pressures and fears. I was told tales of failure and defeat, but I strove on doggedly. I did not have any contemporary examples to follow, but I had received God's revelation and that was enough.

Has not God said in His Word, "But seek ye first the Kingdom of God and his righteousness: and all these things shall be added unto you" –(Matt 6: 33).

What did Jesus mean by "all these things"? Obviously the context reveals that He was referring to the earlier statement. He had commanded thus; "Therefore take no thought, saying, What shall we eat? or, What shall we drink? or Wherewithal shall we be clothed? (For after all these things do the Gentiles seek:) for your heavenly Father knoweth that ye have need of all these things" –(Matt 6:31,32).

The "these things" refer to the necessities that make life comfortable for mankind. They include the best of food, clothes, shelter, mobility, and all. And the good news is that, your heavenly Father knows that you need them, so He will give them as you seek Him first.

I have never approached the preaching of the gospel with a 'grabbing,' or 'get rich' attitude. And I never will! I have done all that which the grace of God would do through me to affect and transform countless lives. It has been accomplished by dint of sheer determination and by God's grace. It has been done through days, weeks, and months of praying and fasting.

I have diligently sowed the whole of my life as a seed in the Kingdom of God by ministering His Word. And I am not ashamed to say that God rewards faithfulness and hard work, regardless of who is involved.

In Paul's second letter to the Corinthians, he stated: "We then, as workers together with him, beseech you also that ye receive not the grace of God in vain" - 6:1. By God's help, I can say I have not received the Lord's grace in vain. I have labored. Yes, I have fought laziness and unbelief. I have aspired for success by the grace of God.

The wisest man who ever lived among men had an admonition for us. In Proverbs 22: 29, King Solomon stated, "Seest thou a man diligent in his business? He shall stand before kings, he shall not stand before mean men." Do you believe God's word? This is true!

One of the errors of our generation is that many ministers of the gospel feel guilty about God's blessing. I do not think I have to apologize for God's blessings merely because I am a pastor: Oh, I do not think so! After all, He has promised to give me "all these things", if I seek first His Kingdom and His righteousness.

God's hand has helped me to build a large fellowship of believers. Many, through the preaching of God's Word and faithful application of divine principles have broken through barriers of poverty to attain great heights of prosperity and abundance. I say this to God's glory. We have come a long way together.

Many members of my church (and I mean a large numbers of them) drive some of the best cars in town to God's glory. What then are you saying? As the Pastor and Apostle of this great work God has established, should I continue to walk the streets of Accra merely to please men? That would not help anybody.

Friend, listen, what society says does not really matter; what God declares is the central factor. You cannot please society; therefore aim at pleasing God.

WRONG CONCEPTS

There are many wrong concepts, which I have abandoned over the years. Honestly speaking, without my knowledge and insight into God's Word, the devil would have taken advantage of my ignorance to destroy God's work and me. But that will not happen!

For several decades Christians have felt that we should have just about enough to eat, inexpensive cars to ride, and the simplest of clothes. To many, that is the way to holiness! Somehow, just somehow, poverty came to mean a sign of true spiritually or some great love for God. But if God decides to bless you, He gives you nothing but the best.

Let me share some insights with you; this will blow all the devil's lies in your mind to shambles. You see, Satan knows that if he keeps the saints shaking in hole-ridden shoes, in rented houses, with unpaid bundles of bills, and hardly enough to eat and get by, then he can effectively stop the spreading of the gospel through books, equipment, international crusades and by satellite, radio, television and other means.

Now, I move to a strong point, which may be distasteful to a few folks. Do you know there may be thousands of Mercedes Benz cars in the nation? Among those who drive and own them are lawyers, bankers, gamblers and prostitutes. Others, like businessmen and diplomats, drive them every day. It may be of interest to note that many cocaine peddlers who have destroyed millions of human lives also drive them on the highways of the nation. Indeed, no one questions why they drive such "posh" cars. Yet society says that the servant of the Most High God should not be anywhere near them. Woe unto the preacher who dares to buy a Benz car or even receives one as a gift for the appreciation for his labors.

The argument raised is that there are needy people in the society and so the man of God should not use the best of things, but give them away to the poor. It sounds appealing, doesn't it?

But listen; we cannot deceive ourselves anymore. In John 12:1-8 we read an interesting episode. All of the twelve apostles were present; surprisingly it was only Judas Iscariot who queried why Mary poured the alabaster oil on Jesus Christ. Judas asked, "Why was not this ointment sold for three hundred pence and given to the poor? This he said, not because he cared for the poor; but because he was a thief, and had the bag" –(John 12:5-6).

The reaction of Jesus Christ to Judas' objection was a radical one. The Lord said, "Let her alone; ...For the poor always ye have with you; but me ye have not always"–(John 12:8). In essence, the full implication of what Jesus Christ meant was that whether the alabaster oil was poured on Him or given to the poor, it would not make the poor poorer or richer, so stop bothering her.

This explanation should settle your worries about the preacher's car. He is building lives by God's Word. The Pastor and Evangelist are transforming lives by the power of the Holy Spirit. Many are they whose lives have been altered for good by the true Bible believing church and its ministers. Suicides have been stopped by prayers and counselling. May God help us see the truth and uphold His Word!

THE MISSIONARIES OF OLD

I believe the other problem the church in Africa has had in relation to prosperity has to do with the approach of missionaries who worked here centuries back. There is no denying that they did and are still doing a tremendous job in evangelism, building hospitals, schools and other social services to make life better for the people. But, sad to say, the missionaries erred tragically by not teaching the Africans God's Word on prosperity, especially where it had to do with the laws regarding Sowing and Reaping.

The reason is not hard to trace. Churches overseas more often then not support the missionaries who work in Africa and elsewhere. Monies, clothing and other essential necessities are sent frequently to them. Other missionaries have monies paid into their home accounts to guarantee a comfortable future. With this background, many missionaries did not have grounds to justify preaching the full counsel of God regarding prosperity through giving, sowing and reaping.

From another point of view, even those who were not supported from their home churches did not have the courage "to say it like it is" from the Bible. Africans generally considered every white man affluent, whether a missionary or not. This atmosphere also produced guilt in the minds of those who tried to preach the full gospel. As a result of this negligence to preach God's prosperity along with other revealed truths, Africans came to assume erroneously that to be a preacher is to be poor.

Thank God it all has to end! He has called us to declare His full counsel to our generation. I preach and teach prosperity like any other doctrine of the Bible.

GIVING AND RECEIVING

I have seen the Word of God change the course of my life and thousands of others. There is one principle I will recommend for you, if you want to stay under the miraculous provision of God, that is GIVING. God's law of Giving and Receiving is clearly stated in Luke 6:38.

Give and it shall be given unto you, good measure, pressed down, and shaken together, and running over, shall men give unto your bosom. For with the same measure that ye mete withal it shall be measured to you again.

Again, in Proverbs 11:24-25 it is written: "There is (he) that scattereth, and yet increaseth, and there is (he) that witholdeth more than is meet, but it tendeth to poverty. The liberal soul shall be made fat: and he that watereth shall be watered also himself."

God's spiritual laws will not change, whether we like it or not. You may be saying right now, "Oh Bishop Nick, you mean I have to start giving my money away if I want to be prosperous? That doesn't make sense." It does! The devil wrote an old concept and engraved it in gold saying. "Get all you can get, hold on to it, keep the lid tight on the can." God's spiritual law says if you scatter your money, it will increase and you will be prosperous. Hoard too much of it, more than is necessary, and you will be poor.

You may read about these biblical principles in Deuteronomy 8:18; 3 John 2; Proverbs 28:19; 2 Thessalonians 3:10; 2 Corinthians 9:6; Galatians 6:9. Take a look at a scripture selection that has transformed the lives of many Christians who adopted God's spiritual law. It is Deuteronomy 28:8.

> *The Lord will command the blessing upon thee in thy storehouses, and in all that thou settest thine hand unto; and he shall bless thee in the land which the LORD thy God giveth thee.*

Verse 2 of the same chapter states that the blessings of the Lord will even "overtake" you. I love that! I have experienced it personally.

Remember this day that no matter how far you are from God's plan of abundance now, when you begin to put God's Word into action, He will overtake you with His blessing. Let God be true!

THAT YOU MAY PROSPER

The world's way of thinking has always baffled me. Now I know that Satan is firmly behind all the deception (Rev. 20:8). Just for a moment, ponder on the points I am about to make. Do you know the ticket fees for boxing tournaments go to pay the boxer's fees? Are you aware that gate fees for football matches help to pay the footballers? It may sound childish to you, but may I ask. "Who gave the hands to the boxer?" It is God the Creator.

Similarly, it is God who gives the skills to the footballer to play with his legs and make a fortune. The Bible actually says "For who maketh thee to differ from another? And what hast thou that didst not receive? Now if thou didst receive it, why dost thou glory, as if thou hadst not received it?" - 1 Cor 4:7.

The intellectual makes a name and fortune by the gift of intelligence and the brilliant brain God endows him with. We now come to the minister of the gospel. God gives His servant grace, anointing, and wisdom to do the work of the ministry in any of the five-fold offices–Apostle, Prophet, Evangelist, Pastor and Teacher–or any other ministry in the church. The servant of God labors in God's Word and prays to succeed. And when God blesses His servant's ministry, the whole world rises in condemnation.

It is needful to clarify a few points. The Bible says in Psalm 24:1, "The earth is the LORD'S and the fullness thereof; the world, and they that dwell therein."

For the avoidance of doubt on ownership, God said in Haggai 2:8, "The silver is mine, and the gold is mine, saith the LORD of hosts."

By direct interpretation, what the two scripture verses imply is that God owns the earth as well as the gold, silver, diamond and all in the earth. Therefore it stands to reason that all human beings, including doctors, lawyers, engineers, and gold miners succeed and prosper at the expense of God's created wealth and other natural deposits in the earth.

On this score, it would be unfair, unjust and a direct con-tradiction of God's Word for society or any group of people to deprive anyone of the fruits of his lawful labor. The Bible says in Ephesians 4:28; "Let him that stole steal no more: but rather let him labor, working with his hands the thing which is good, that he may have to give to him that needeth."

Any individual who works hard, uses his or her God-given talents and resources, and abides within the limits of the law, is entitled to receive the blessings of his or her labor. No one should be deprived of God's blessings.

It does not matter what you think: God's Word stands. I believe that God has raised me as a leader and an example to my generation about His goodness, mercy and prosperity. I do always remember from where God picked me. Like David, He took me from the backside and placed His grace upon me. This, He did so that I can be a reference point to those who need the grace of God. It does not matter what the world says, God will show you favor in due time.

May the God and father of our Lord Jesus Christ visit you with His power and prosperity in every way of life as you act on the words of this book? "Keep therefore the words of this covenant, and do them, that ye may prosper in all that you do." –(Deut 29:9).

If you stand on God's Word, God promises will stand with you, as He told Abraham in Genesis 12:3, "And I will bless them that bless thee, and curse him that curseth thee:"